LIFE SENTENCES

LIFE SENTENCES

WRITINGS FROM INSIDE AN AMERICAN PRISON

*Written by Malakki (Ralph Bolden), Oscar Brown, Khalifa
(Richard Diggs), Fly (James Martin), Charles "Shawn"
Robinson, Faruq (Robert Wideman)*

*Edited by Norm Conti, Amber Epps, Elaine Frantz,
Michelle Grissom, Nechama Weingart*

Introduction by Amber Epps

Afterword by John Edgar Wideman

Illustrations by Christine Lorenz

Belt Publishing

Belt Publishing
3143 West 33rd Street, #6
Cleveland, Ohio 44109
www.beltpublishing.com

Cover art and book design by David Wilson

To Khalifa, who challenged and inspired
us with his love and rage

CHAPTER THREE: PRISON LIFE

CHAPTER FOUR: RESTORATION

AFTERWORD: LAST DAY **159**

ABOUT THE WRITERS AND EDITORS **167**

INTRODUCTION

I don't want to write this. Just like I didn't want to go to that spaghetti dinner at that church that was raising money to help my brother pay for the college courses he wanted to take. I sat at that table with my family eating food I didn't want, pretending to be emotionally strong enough to deal with the smiling faces of strangers who somehow had it in their hearts to put this thing together. I held back tears and swallowed them with every bite of pasta while one of the women from the church reminded me, for the 72nd time, not to forget to get a piece of cake or something from the dessert table. I didn't want dessert. I didn't want to be there. Yet, there I was, voluntarily, yet feeling like I had no choice but to be there. On the table was a reserved sign that said "Brother O's Family." Noticing that sign is what made me recognize that I was being held against my will, almost a hostage situation, being forced to be in a place I'm not comfortable, with people I don't know, eating food that I don't prefer.

For a number of years during his incarceration, my brother was housed at the State Correctional Institution in Pittsburgh, also known as SCI Pittsburgh, Western Penitentiary, or "The Wall." This facility was built along the Ohio River in 1883 with forced prison labor, and, as it still stands, continues to look like a fortress.

Made out of massive stone blocks and iron bars, the facility sits on a river that looks as cold, uninviting, and even deadly as the building itself. It was here that my brother and a number of others serving very long sentences, one of which was finite while the others had been given life without the possibility of parole because they had been convicted of homicide or felony homicide (participating in a felony during which someone committed homicide), came together to form an extremely powerful group. Before incarceration, all of these men lived within ten miles of the prison. These six men—Robert "Faruq" Wideman, James "Fly" Martin, Richard "Khalifa" Diggs, Ralph "Malakki" Bolden, Oscar Brown, and Clarence "Shawn" Robinson—are the authors of this book. Sadly, Khalifa died of complications related to late-diagnosed cancer, apparently alone on the floor of a hospital bathroom, while his family and friends tried desperately to get information about where he had been taken, on December 7, 2017. He left behind hundreds of writings that give great insight into his life, his loves, his laughters, and his laments, some of which you will read in this book. The other men continue to live physically behind the walls of the prisons that they were transferred to after the closing of SCI Pittsburgh in 2017. Although physically confined, these men have found ways to rise above those walls through reading, religion, classes, writing, and both learning from and teaching other inmates with whom they live.

These men, the authors of this book, came together in 2011 to form the Elsinore Bennu Think Tank, along with Remi Annunziata, Norm Conti, Elaine Frantz, Rob Klein, Maggie McGannon, and Stephen Stept, who came into the prison from the outside. The Think Tank met every Friday morning, and a lot of teaching and learning took place. The direction that the group took was one of Restorative Justice, which is a type of criminal justice that focuses on rehabilitating offenders by repairing the harm done to not only the victims, but also the greater community, while addressing the social circumstances that led to the crime itself. Many were invited to visit or join the group, and anyone who felt so inclined to become a part was welcomed. Faruq's brother, novelist John Edgar Wideman, was one such visitor. Other visitors included Robert Ellsberg, a Catholic social radical; faculty, students, and administrators from Duquesne University such as Lina Dostillio; and activists and political leaders from the Pittsburgh area and beyond, including Inside Out founders Lori Pompa and Tyrone Werts.

Members of the group wrote, and wrote, and wrote some more over the years, and read their writings to each other at the meetings. At some point they asked Elaine and Norm to help them put the writings together to form a book—this book—that in a way, had already been forming itself. Elaine and Norm set up an editorial group outside the prison that included people who had various skills, insights, and other contributions to offer. The group consisted of myself, Michele Grissom (Khalifa's daughter), Nechama Weingart, Christina Lorenz, and Maggie McGannon. We met on Sundays at Elaine's house. During these meetings we pored through the piles of writings that the men had given us, looking for common themes and trying to figure out how to best organize their ideas, thoughts, knowledge, and experiences in a way that would make sense to a reader. We also had to figure out a design for the book, and then identify a publisher that would be interested in producing something of this nature. Luckily, Grant Olson was there to make us lunch on those days. Food not only brings people together, but can also help keep them grounded. Goodness knows that I needed grounding. I often found myself quiet and trying not to cry, which would have caused me to choke on my lunch, as I looked at the writings of these men—these intelligent, loving, self-aware, caring, honest men who, because of a poor choice made in their youth, were sentenced to live out the rest of their lives behind bars and barbed wire. While most of the men wrote their essays, poems, and narratives on typewriters, my brother, Oscar, wrote his by hand. Looking at his large, sloppy handwriting brought on the unwanted reminder that my baby brother, Brother O, Oscar Brown, Oscar Eugene Brown III, has been "living" in a place where he's not comfortable, with people he doesn't know, eating food he doesn't prefer. Sentenced to life plus 10 to 20 years, in 2006. He was nineteen years old. And there was nothing I could do about it.

During the editorial process, the group often reached out to the men to ask for their guidance and feedback, and sometimes additional writings. They were excited about this book, interested in the process, and eagerly awaited its completion. In speaking with my brother on the phone about the book, I could hear the anticipation and enthusiasm in his voice. He would say, "Yeah, I got an email from Elaine asking me to write something else, but I don't know what to write." Then I would hear from him again and he would say, "I wrote something else and sent it to Elaine. I hope she got it!" Finally, he and the other members of the Elsinore Bennu Think Tank had a way to make their voices heard outside of the walls inside which they were confined. It was a project. A real life project that their names would be on. A chance to be heard and be taken seriously. In essence, this was a way for them to "get out of jail"…free.

Keeping in alignment with the idea of restorative justice, this book has four chapters, each one centered around the different phases of the process. Chapter One includes writings that describe the men's lives before they were incarcerated. While their lives may have been considered untraditional to outsiders, the men detail experiences they had and situations they found themselves in that were not necessarily out of the ordinary for the communities in which they resided. What's abnormal to one may be completely normal to another. The next chapter provides insight into the moments when their lives changed and they found themselves involved in committing a crime, being arrested, taken to trial, and finally, incarcerated. Disruption. The third chapter explores how the men, although in prison, began to rebuild their lives, developing meaningful relationships inside the prison while also working to reconnect and rebuild with their families and friends on the outside. The writings in the fourth and final chapter revolve around the men's realizations that working together to better their communities outside the prison is the only way they could experience true healing and freedom. Restorative Justice.

Most times after leaving the editorial sessions, I found myself depressed for days at a time, thinking about these men that I came to know through their writings as more than just inmates. I developed such a strong sense of what they could be doing had they been given a second chance. I wanted to go get them and take them back to their communities so they could continue to teach, rebuild, mentor, and offer support as they do for fellow inmates, but on the outside. I can't stop imaging the impact they could have. For a person who is used to having control over most things in their life, not having control over this situation is an extremely defeating, helpless feeling. Although I am not able to drive to the prison and demand that my brother be released, I was able to be a part of this process, helping him and the others climb the walls of the prison through the publication of these works.

I hope that those who read this book are able to gain insight. Having a better understanding of each other, creating greater levels of acceptance, and working toward restoring and rebuilding relationships and communities that have been broken, are first steps in enacting much-needed change. The fact that these men, sentenced to live out most, if not the rest, of their lives, were able to find a way to become free is amazing, motivational, inspirational. The rest of us could learn a lot from them.

—Amber Epps

cla   ra
oli   ull
per   in i
le   of co
ro   Jesus
            rds to aga
            cy yearnings
            on.   We a
        k of human ad.
        e rear, watching   t
    you   as quick to murder th
stead   ery, or jim crow viol.
gove   or/lack of patriotis
pla   round" shit, you kill
a   fear(s). Or your
                ficed
    Your lynchings now come at
felt threatened" well I got
fe for no reason except som
not scared of you no mo
Philadelphia, where you
yall went to jail!
despite the num
thyou know
because my people we
sted   for the infam
its filed long after mo
o you want to talk abo
ove upon police train
binding rules, they did
see, I know this is again so
they'll come around at the mention
ccompanied with a promise. But theres
ing that rhetoric because t
this has been a thought out
ne modern tactics of application have
e racism.   the fear / and the crimi
genocide of people of color remai
at a   for a white system of god players
period for a white system of god players
certai   ou don't want to talk about injusti
on rugs law (otherwise known as legalized hunting
color & poor) for sure you don't want to discuss mass in
you've found the need for public safety to disguise your assau
of unarmed black youth! I'm convinced of your sickness when
was more important to close schools and build more prisons _
yo   to re write laws to increase criminal law codes

CHAPTER I
LIFE

FOUND MEMORIES # 1 / Fly

I remember when my father used to take my brother and me fishing. My brother and I couldn't sleep the night before—we'll be up talking about all the fish that we was going to catch the next day.

Till my mother would come in the room and tell us quit talk and go to bed. She'll say, "you know that you boys will be getting up in about three hours and if you not ready your father will leave you." But he never left us. That was her way of making us go to bed.

We used to get up about 3:30 or 4:00. My father liked to get on the road early. First, we would stop by Mr. Herman's house to get him. My father must've called him before we left the house, because he would always be waiting for us on his porch. When he got in the car, one of the first things he would always say to me and my brother was, "Who's going to catch the biggest fish today?" And me and my brother would say at the same time, "me, me, me", and Mr. Herman would just laugh.

We would go to different places to fish all the time, like Lake Arthur, Lake Wilhelm, Moraine State Park, or some pay lakes my father liked.

My father used to say the best time to fish was early in the mornings. So we would get there early and set up the fishing rods. My father taught me and my brother how to put the worms, corn, and dough on the rods, how to throw the rods in the water, how to watch the water and see the change in how the water moves when the fish are biting and how to reel them in.

My mother would pack a picnic basket for us for lunch. We would stay till about 4:00 or 5:00 that afternoon. Sometimes we would listen to the Pittsburgh Pirates game on the radio. A lot of the fish that we caught we would put back in the water. Sometimes we would take the fish home with us.

It was just a lot of fun for me and my brother to be out fishing with our father.

FOUND MEMORIES # 2 / Fly

I remember back in 1981. I went to the Stanley Theatre in downtown Pittsburgh to see a Rick James concert. At that time, I thought that I was God's gift to all women. I used to wear tuxedos or suits to all the concerts. I also used to wear my hair in curls. So I'm at the concert sitting in the front row enjoying myself, and Rick James looks at me and says, "Hey you, nigger in that white tuxedo. Where the hell do you think you at? You ain't at no after-prom. We came here to funk."

Before he played his last three songs, someone came up to me saying that Rick wanted to see me after the show. So when I went backstage, the first thing he said to me was "Motherfucker, what made you wear a tuxedo to my show? Are you trying to show me up?" and start laughing. We start talking and hit it off so that night me Rick and a couple of guys from his band hung out. We started out by going to Bob's Auto Pub. That was a bar in Market Square, in downtown Pittsburgh. From there we went to the Commercial Club that was located on Fifth Ave in the Hill District.

We partied till about 4:00 a.m. After that, we went to his hotel along with about six woman and continued to party, and yes, it's true that Rick got high a lot. I thought I liked to get high, but I was not in his league. I left Rick about 2:00 p.m. the next day.

That was not the last time that I would hang out with Rick. But I will never forget the first time.

SCRATCH POETS / Malakki

Scratch Poets was an invention by me and the venerable Christian X (R.I.P.), but the idea of us coming together came from a local director who caught me DJing a party and asked me to add some music and play a small part in a movie he was doing in the city. When he came to my place to see what I did, I showed him more of me. For I was not just a DJ but a performance artist: a sound alchemist stealing pieces from various everythings (from *The Munsters* TV show to recording rain storms) to produce aural gold.

He told me there was a poet who would pair perfectly with what I was doing. When Chris and I met, the revolution began. He was a most terrific, gifted poet. But it wasn't his fault. He simply gave voice to the tragic persona that tortured his inner being. I loved him and wish he didn't kill himself because he helped me turn pieces of me and catch phrases scribbled on scrap paper into poetry. This made me a triple-threat: DJ, producer, and poet.

Sometimes I would do music for other artists, and I really liked what the new street artists brought to the rap genre and the rich texture existing when they layered their gritty stories about the streets with perfect rhyme and meter seen only before in Shakespearean sonnets. Some of my poetry had reflected this but the unfortunate downside to becoming more intimate with their understanding was that I was influenced by them to "keep it real" and not just be about talk. I had walked on the wild side occasionally, but as my anxiety and other issues I was dealing with got worse, I began to indulge more and more into the dark side of the streets. It felt like I found the perfect place to hide and less light brought comfort to the pushed-down digression of my self-esteem. As the anxiety took hold of me, becoming more confrontational and ready to fight brought smiles and pleasing nods to the new circle that adopted me. Scratch Poets became secondary to this new crew of discontents. It got worse from there. The best way to explain it is Proverbs 14:12: "There is a way which seemeth right unto a man, but the end thereof are the ways of death."

DOING DIRT / Oscar

My life pre-prison was pretty much normal. I held a job and the only exception was, I sold drugs on the side. I would work 8:00 a.m.–4:00 p.m. Monday through Friday, and once out of work I would sell drugs. Cocaine: heroin to be exact. I also carried guns and occasionally if something fell in my lap would rob people. Gentleman by day. Gangster by night. Oh yeah, smoked a lot of weed in between. That is pretty much all I did. Prison was no surprise because I did a whole lot of shit and got caught up and boom. So yeah I'm keepin' it 100% with this and it is what it is. I had to defend myself and someone was killed unfortunately; someone who I knew for a long time who was also into the same exact shit I was into. Criminal on criminal. I shouldn't have been involved in what I was involved in but I was and when you do dirt you eat dirt and I'm eating dirt.

MY VERY YOUNG YEARS / Khalifa

I was born in McKeesport. My very young years are marred with glimpses only of childhood, rendering much the same story of practically all poor black people in that era (the 1950s). Only I (we) didn't know we were poor, because everybody around us lived pretty much under the same conditions. Our house was in what was then called the First Ward, right next to Edgar Thomson Steel Works: I guess you can imagine the constant stench of burning or melting steel, and the coal trucks roaring back and forth all day, everyday, and the railroad train of which railroad tracks were approximately 30 feet from our house. Between the smoke-filled stack pipes—the horns of trains and the traffic of unfamiliar faces moving to and fro, there was a beer garden on two of the three corners that formed the junction of Water Street and Market, which we had to walk daily to attend school (Market Street School), that was once a Catholic rectory! By the way, I was born with bronchial asthma, so my condition often made it difficult for me to keep up with the kids my age. Which turned out at first to be alright cause it was the perfect excuse to be around adults all the time. However, that soon became a nightmare in terms of abuse (not sexually imposed on my body, as opposed to my young body being subject to fill in for husbands working late nights in the mill, or when some of the older ladies flashed memories of how they used to be loved and touched, kissed).

Unfortunately, the city's water sewage company was about three-quarters of a block away from where our house was, so every time they would flush the system we would get the brunt of the smell, depending on how strong the wind was blowing and in which direction!

The Youghiogheny and Monongahela: when it would rain real hard and flood we'd have to go to my Aunt's house up on Jennylind! Eventually we moved over on Water Street, a mere two blocks from where we were originally, but at least out of imminent danger of floods! Al Duffy's tavern was on the corner of the street. On the weekends it was always jumpin'. Most of the black mill workers had bills in there so it was packed with them every weekend and the prostitutes would make sure to be easily located from Thursday to Sunday! It was a lesson as well a nightmare! Fights were always happening, dudes over women, women being accused of stealing drunks' money, strong armed robberies of white dudes that came to buy that black gold (women). That time was a blur for real, between hospital trips and being babysitted by some older lady who wanted to not be "doing anything that afternoon" (while my mother had to go to the welfare office, in its rhythm and decadence that was seemingly unseen and accepted!)

Sometime in the mid-fifties, Harrison Village Projects was built, we had moved from First Ward to Water Street to Railroad Street—to Market Street and now was waiting for placement in the newly built projects. We felt like the Jeffersons, movin' on up! I was three—going on nine, and I felt fifteen! I had seen things and been accused of things, learned to steal, lie and play absolutely dumb!

In the course of these migratory moves, my family had dwindled from ten members to seven. I was the youngest of the seven boys and three sisters. Seven of us had reached the projects: four boys, a baby-sister, and moms and pop. The projects provided a new life-- a more cohesive life, a more congested life, everybody knew everybody's business--the cheating husbands, the wandering wives, the next-door lovers, and all the drifting single women just trying to feed their children and there were plenty of children in Harrison Village!

Ironically, our building was approximately twenty to twenty-five feet away from the river, the Yough. Damn, I thought we were rid of floods and found out quite fearfully that we were at a far greater danger, coupled with the rats coming up off the banks to escape the often floods in McKeesport. I'd seen rats in the First Ward, but they were not so offensive as these. It's like these projects rats had no fear! They were bigger it seemed, and so stomping your feet and screamin' didn't mean anything, except to let them know you were scared, and that seemed to make them bolder! They'd just sit there and look at you—like you were in the wrong place messing up their groove! Eventually they became our personal prey, and we used trapping techniques which later enhanced our spy game on the people who we decided were worth following and robbing. These practices often determined whether or not we ate junk food: candy, sodas, and chips were not on the family food shopping list because of minimal income. Family treats were usually gotten from the welfare surplus warehouse on the first Monday of the month, and most likely they were sugar-coated cereals! Yeah, we hustled pop-bottles and ran store errands for the elders, we even cut grass and shoveled snow, but that was considered "work for treats," and that money was hard earned!

I was eight, and around this time began seeing white people on somewhat of a consistent basis. I had begun hospital treatments for my asthma condition, which consisted of a variety of allergy shots to see what I was allergic to. Usually twelve shots every other Monday—six in each arm. The dizzying smell of G. C. Murphys' perfume on these white nurses seem to nauseate me even beyond my fear of needles, and I was usually given a tootsie roll or sucker to counteract any ill feeling about the blood oftentimes that would run down my shirt sleeves from an innocent (I guess) too- soon withdrawal of the needle. It was a whole new world to me, because I was barely used to seeing European people! My world was black, with the exception of a few white (poor) kids going to Market Street School, the only other faces were like mine! I saw those same faces when we would go shopping on payday, but they acted like they never saw us!

My mother would always say things like "thank you" and "no sir," but they would say shit like, "Here you are, dear," or "Those children are so mannerly and cute, are they yours?" I heard, but didn't understand the underlying difference in dialect until years later, and that only served to embitter me more when they talked at me. Cause I never felt they were talking with or to me, but to a something!

While memory is blurry, times were peaceful—good in fact, when you consider no one was above the other. We were all functioning well, considering the conditions of life unfolding for us. You would see fathers down Murray field running races with the kids, mothers sitting on stoops plaiting hair, older dudes sipping wine and singing in an attempt to lure the attention of one of the older ladies just sitting outside watching who's who! Sometimes when the ice cream truck would roll around, some hustler or preacher or pimp would be on the scene and invite all the children over to the truck and buy cones for us all. No one would be left out, and we had to wait till all the little girls got theirs first. As a matter of fact, we always had to be seen treating the girls with respect and politeness. Otherwise, there'd be consequences, reprimand, parents told, maybe even a butt-whopping, demands to know who it was that saw the misbehaving. But it was all in good intent!

School was okay, but I never really felt comfortable going. All too many times I remember not getting new school clothes, instead I was given the hand-me-downs from my brother Tommy who was a year older than me. They weren't raggedy clothes, and for sure pressed and clean, but I knew, and sometimes someone would ask "didn't your brother have a shirt like that?" or, flat out, "is that your brother's?" I had no real connection with embarrassment, but I remember the feeling of being singled out and laughed at. But in project life, the joke today could always be played on the joker of yesterday. Sure enough, what went around came around, so we all kinda just capped on each other, knowing our day was coming. We were all poor and in need of something sooner or later, it was a joke on us, a way of lessening the pain of poverty. Today, they call it "desynthesizing."

MY LIFE / Shawn

My mother had me when she was sixteen and my dad was twenty. My dad went to prison when I was four and did not get out until I was twenty-four. He did twenty years straight. I grew up with a sister and two brothers, all younger than me. I am the only one who has ever been in trouble with the law. I was raised with a stepfather, one of my brothers' father. I witnessed my stepfather and mother fighting once when I was about eight or nine. She divorced him right after that, but I stayed to live with him because he would not let my mother take his son and my little brother wanted me to stay with him. My sister left with my mom. My youngest brother had not been born just yet.

At first, when I was like eight years old, I wanted to be a lawyer. Because my mother would always complain about me "talking too much" and said I needed a job where I can talk for a living. My mother was dealing with a court issue, and her lawyer would always come to the house. He would talk to my mother for hours, and that was when I said to my mother that I wanted to be a lawyer. Then as I got older I was very involved in doing art. Drawing and painting. I even sent away for that art contest that was in the back of magazines. The one where you would draw the parrot or the pirate.

When I was younger, I spent a lot of time at the Boys Club during the summer and I would do arts and crafts. I was good at drawing, and thought I would work somewhere doing some form of art, but being that my family was not "rich," my mother and stepfather would provide what we "needed" and not everything we "wanted". So, living in the suburbs I was "hustling" by cutting grass in the summer and shoveling snow in the winter.

I started selling marijuana when I was fourteen. Right around that time, I started liking girls. I really didn't like school all that much. I dropped out at sixteen and went to Job Corps in

Chesapeake Bay, Maryland. That wasn't what I thought it was. I stayed there for nine months before getting kicked out for fighting because of some girl's boyfriend who didn't like that his girlfriend liked me. My dreams of becoming an artist or lawyer went out the window because I didn't have the patience to earn money the "correct" way, by working for a living. After the Corps I started breaking into stores. Stealing cars, breaking into stores, and selling drugs became easy to me. Being that I was well-liked and knew how to deal with people, it was easy to cross over to the criminal side. Do you remember back in 1987 and 1988 when Pittsburgh was dealing with what the news was calling "smash and grab" burglaries? Well I was a part of that. Mostly Radio Shacks were being hit. You could probably research and find info about that because it was big news back then. My burglary crew was known as the "Whylie Avenue Hustlers" from the Hill District.

I went to prison for three years in 1988 because of that case. I was released in 1991. At first, I started out well. I was enrolled in the Art Institute of Pittsburgh and worked at Giant Eagle where I met my daughter's mother. I started selling drugs in 1992, up until I came to prison in December 1993 for my homicide case. I've been in prison ever since.

While selling drugs I always wanted to get out of the drug game and buy property to fix up and sell. That was my plan before I was caught up in this crime. The money I made from selling drugs went to attorney's fees and then, after my conviction, my daughter's mother kept what was left. She sold my cars and lived off of the money that was left for about five years, plus also taking care of my needs in prison. I never thought I would end up in prison again after that first time, but poor choices and a major mistake.

Now I'm fighting to get "my life" back.

LIFE / Faruq

The first time I remember realizing John was someone other than just my brother was around 1963, when *Life* magazine came to our home, our poor old house on Marchand Street in the East Liberty section of Pittsburgh, to take pictures. At the time, *Life* was one of the biggest selling national weekly magazines. John had been awarded the highly prestigious, academically acclaimed Rhodes scholarship. He was already in college, winning basketball championships, but in my young eyes just my oldest brother. Not someone famous, just John. But I was twelve years old, and *Life* magazine was coming to our home. Wow! Now that was exciting.

Mom had done everything humanly possible to, as she would say, "make the house look presentable." This included pushing my sister, Letisha, my two brothers, Otis and David, and me to clean and polish every crack and crevice in the house. As usual, I tried ducking most of the work. At twelve, I had already developed an overblown sense of self. Mom again: "that boy's just so dam full of himself." I did not understand it intellectually, but I was developing the bad habits that would lead to my self-destruction. Looking for the easier, softer way, wanting maximum results with minimum effort.

I wrongly convinced myself early on that charm and quick wit worked well for me. I put maximum effort into practicing those techniques and became good at being manipulative and deceitful. What we live we learn. What we learn we practice. What we learn we become. Despite the admonishments and good examples of my mother, father, and older siblings, weekly church attendance, and a few caring teachers, I still pursued the ways of the con man. A fool and a baby and I didn't even know it. I thought I was clever and grown even at twelve, and for many years to come. Eventually my inability to respect or expect the authority of the institutions that hold our society together would lead to my rebellious destruction. This rebellion was also based on emotional and societal forces I reacted to although I did not yet completely comprehend race and money's hold on power.

So *Life* magazine was coming to do a story on brother John receiving a Rhodes scholarship. Him and another young black man were the first blacks to be awarded the prestigious scholarship. *Life* and *Look* magazines were noted for their big glossy pictures using the latest technology. Everywhere, all over America, people sat them on their coffee tables. It was the latest trend. In 1963 with the simplicity of a child I thought people all over the country might have a picture of us sitting on their coffee table.

In 1963 and throughout that decade, black people—who were still negroes at the time, still ambivalent whether we were black, colored, negro, Afro-American, African-American—would have many firsts and popular media would cover them all. America was experiencing social, political, and racial upheaval, and people were demanding change. White America and its Northeastern media centers were experiencing a new mixed sense of guilt and early attempts of political correctness. Media was not as politically and racially sophisticated as it is now. At that time, they awarded and announced all these firsts with pride in their own ability to be magnanimous rather than congratulating the recipients for the extra effort required. The country was patting itself on the back, celebrating its magnanimity, living up to its creed 400 years overdue. Most black folk still lived the nightmare of separation, inequality and dispossession in the land of our birth. The marginal gestures of letting one escape or break into the dominant society left us pleased and confused yet curiously with a bitter taste. Most of us applauded the changes and appreciated being recognized. However, collectively, we remained left with dreams deferred.

John would continue making headlines for his positive accomplishments. The first negro to—the first black to—the first

Afro-American to—the first African American to. Times changed and we as a people changed our name in search of an identity stolen and beaten out of us by 400 years of slavery, Jim Crow, segregation, integration, assimilation and finally amelioration by divesting us of our last vestiges of culture or any prideful connections to a motherland or history. Collectively we were awarded with being the first blacks to be white. Hurrah, our day has arrived. Please excuse the delirium of a lost people.

SEE ME / Khalifa

Wasn't a damn thing recognizable to me except the Man-Power office building that was across the street from Shaw Avenue Grade School. Prior to my being sentenced to Thorn-Hill Institution, I was attending Walnut Street School and knew everybody in the school. After all, we mostly lived in the projects and hung out together. Well, we had cliques of course, but Harrison Village had its own identity, and we rode on that. Everybody was scraping to get by but we didn't know the difference—because no one stood above the other. There was someone in every section that drank, or worked in the mill, or was on welfare, or in many cases both. Most tenants were actually married, but all their husbands had mill-weekend-girlfriends! There were constantly people coming up from the South staying for like a summer and then disappearing again. The same with folk from Cleveland, Ohio. They were usually kinda young and fine so we made it our business to befriend them.

I had about four months to go before graduating from Shaw and moving on to junior high—at least I hoped. It had become somewhat of a joke that I'd even be home to start a school year. More often than not I was asked: Did I run away from some joint, or am I home on some type of extended summer vacation? I wasn't bad, more delinquent than anything, full of curiosity and a little too much heart for a little guy. Up to this point I hadn't really hurt anyone—aside from fistfights, which I too received some scars, black eyes, and missing teeth. But it was that kind of space we were all in, basically a four-block square that everything happened in. Unless of course we decided to go to Kennywood Park or Eden-Park Roller Rink. And truthfully speaking, we all were quite country. At least that's how I was accepted in the juvenile joints I had been in, and by this time I had several trips to juvenile court, a camp for wayward youth called Sleepy-Hollow, a foster home, a transit home, and Thorn Hill.

But now, standing in the schoolyard of Shaw Avenue was actually the first time I felt I was somewhere I didn't belong. Of course there were a few white kids in those institutions, but for the most part you could tell they were some welfare dudes too. Besides, they were pretty game as far as getting into trouble. But these cats out here with me now in this schoolyard were clearly a different breed: they had school bags, and nice tan pants with blue shirts and shinned loafers—haircuts and you could hear some jingle in their pockets. But I didn't know none of them and that felt really strange—to me.

I wandered over by this huge black chain that cordoned off the teachers' parking lot and stood by myself. They were running past me laughing and tagging each other as if I wasn't even standing there. I watched one dude try jumping the chain barrier and not quite getting his lead foot high enough and bite the asphalt! Damn, he hit kinda hard mostly because he didn't know how to break his fall or roll with it. I mean, he just hit—splat. A couple kids came over after he didn't get right back up and stood looking at him, until finally he rolled over and sat up. A little blood now showing through his pretty little blue shirt; his knee was sorta scraped but no real damage as far as I could see. Raising his arm, I could see he was wiping away what looked like some tears about to fall, and some little black-haired girl asked was he okay. He shook his head, got up with the help of two of his buddies and hobbled over to the steps leading inside the school. I guessed he was going to the nurse's room and get some attention. I thought to myself, "Shit, that's a story on the corner tonight!" And then it hit me: no one said two words to me! I mean, I was standing no more than two feet from the entire incident, and they acted like I wasn't even there! No "Excuse me", "Hey, are you new here?"; "What's your name?"; "What grade you in?" Instead I felt like one of those black jockeys you see on the lawns of the homes up by the library. I felt invisible—and I felt alone. I felt naked, because I didn't even have my first knife with me to back my often smart-ass mouth with. I was known for saying stuff if I thought you were playing past me or ignoring me, actually I would just feel inferior and want to make a statement because I am here! I am real.

I heard another bell go off in the school, and it was the notice that another grade was coming out to the yard. I stood looking at the door hoping to see some familiar face, even someone I didn't get along with would have been okay for right now. Plus, it would give me a chance to holler across the yard and to call to attention: I'm alive, I'm not the colored landscape piece planted to designate the parking lot. I am breathing and now plotting on getting a couple of you real happy punks for your lunch money just because you don't see me!

Out of the doors came my relief, wearing over-ironed and out-of-season corduroy pants and a pressed banlon shirt that shouldn't have been ironed in the first place, but that was my partner Donnie Ray. "Yo! Donnie—Donnie, what's happening?" He was equally glad to see me too, not that he didn't know some of the kids in the yard. This was the first day he'd seen me without a family member with me since I had gotten home from the joint. We greeted each other with the slapping of hands and the giving of five—cause that's what separated cool dudes from squares you know. Now I had the comfort zone that allowed me to take a cigarette out and light up. (A Lucky Strike! One of my Dad's, of course.) I know I was feeling better because I sort of hitched up my pants. I felt rather naked before his arrival, and as we were talking and he was briefing me on the targets, Greg came out and he spotted us first hollering and putting that strutty walk down crossing the yard to us. Ah, finally a shirt now, that was starched and obviously catching the eye of the yard. Greg was a sho-nough country boy, unusually strong for his age and size, big lips and head, stocky built and always ready to fight. And here he was calling and coming over to me! It's on now! I could see the cats looking wondering: "Who is that? What's his name? How he know Donnie and Greg? Is he like them?" Needless to say, when the bell rang again that was our sign to slide away and head downtown. It wasn't but a block away and wouldn't nobody miss us. And it would give me a chance to catch up on what this school is about and what vulnerable honeys were on the limb.

Naturally, we walked towards the state store and after a few minutes saw Bubba. We pitched in and bought two quarts of muscatel wine and went up to Water Street, stopping briefly at Barb's store and buying some Juicy Fruit gum. We crossed Water Street, hopped the fence and went down on the riverbank and cracked the wine. Damn, it felt good to be with my own cats I had run the streets with, stuck up drunks with, pulled trains on girlies under the stairwell in the projects, and hustled stolen goods from downtown. They were better than my brothers to me. And so I thought it only fitting I put them down with some cats I had met in Thorn Hill but lived where they called the city! I told them they were some cool cats from Homewood, some I'd known from living in East Liberty (but hadn't seen) since being displaced back in the Port, and from Northside. Although they were eager to hear the stories of times I had run away from the joint with these cats, they still had reservations about coming to Pittsburgh with me on the weekend. But it was good to see them, especially at the same school I was placed in. I knew it was going to be fun-filled three or four months of hustling, bullying, and new girls who sought out titles for hangin' with the knowing bad boys!

I knew in my mind I was gonna make them pay for not seeing me, for not speaking to me, for acting like I wasn't there or had some disease. Truth is I hadn't took a deep breath yet, everything was shallow, quick, and numb. I guess the only thing that stood out in my mind is that I didn't feel alive. I didn't feel like anyone cared, or that anyone even knew what was happening to me—inside me! Hell, I didn't know myself and couldn't have explained it if someone were to ask.

A BULLET AND A PRAYER / Malakki

I tried to write something positive and wise,
but then I'm mourning because another black child dies.
Another black family shares their sorrow and cries,
and I'm surrounded by black men with no tomorrow in their eyes.
GO
to our neighborhoods, it's like justice
STOPS
here,
although we walk through the streets in the position of TAKBIR.
Hands up,
but we still get shot here,
still get shocked, and choked-out non-stop here.
We can walk through the streets in protest,
still get gunned down bloody as used Kotex.
If you want to march, the peace sign's the best sign language,
it's giving the middle finger to trigger fingers that cause
black anguish.
Are cops addicted to the trigger?
They can't wait to pull it,
then fear floats like a shell case, hate stings like the bullet.
We try to blast back with non-violent actions,
from Crispus Attucks to George Jackson; still no satisfaction.
From Emmett Till, Trayvon Martin, to Michael Brown,
and you claim I'm violent when I burn shit down.
Eric Garner couldn't breathe like he was trapped in a Ziplock,
they still lynch black men; a cop's grip is the slipknot.
R.I.P.
'cause from the rip,
their hands are on the heat on their hips,
with an ice-cold stare that goes back to slave ships.
Like Santa, "post-racial" is a myth that keeps on living,

while Black Hate is a gift that America keeps on giving.
Because when police come to release their fury,
their trigger finger's the judge, the bullets are the jury.
The "bang-bang" is not the gavel, but the stainless steel,
the scales of justice lean like
a kid on training wheels.
Showing us that
black lives don't matter, the system doesn't care,
black men get incarcerated or get
a bullet, then a prayer.

In Memorium to Unarmed Black Men and Children Killed by
the Police:
Amadou Diallo
Patrick Dorismond
Orlando Barlow
Johnny Gammage
Michael Ellerbee
Ousmane Zongo
Timothy Stansbury
Sean Bell
Ramarley Graham
Steven Eugene Washington
Wendell Allen
Kendrec McDade
Victor Steen
Timothy Russell
Jonathan Ferrell
John Crawford
Akai Gurley
Michael Brown
Tamir Rice
Eric Garner

A GANGSTA AND A GENTLEMAN / Oscar

Should I bury you after all we've been through? I can't just turn my back like that after all those nights in the trap busting snaps. Remember when Cricket first came out? You used that weed money to grab that phone, and now it was on no more pager; hustle off the phone. Now you were good—could buy better clothes and shorties would notice you—but before it was like you had the flu. But who knew what a little cash would do?

The gentleman was always there full of care to those he loved, tried to do the right thing, and get A JOB. But the burning desire of the streets was hot. So you got off work and hit the block—had to show my face to stay relevant. The gentleman felt nicely sometimes. I could let my guard down, but it would soon wear off. It's like a wolf being a sheep until he gets the itch and has to scratch it. You loved the thug life running around at night with no worries, but that was a lie because the homie died of a homicide. I dodged that one and realized the gangsta is not always so fun.

The gentleman always treated his girl with the utmost respect but the gangsta did the same, so maybe these two were not so different. You struggled with the gentleman but found comfort in the gangsta. Which one is harder to wear? Make your mind up and try to wear that suit like an average Joe and leave that gangsta behind, but it's hard—because he made me—me.

To some it's easy to see who I should be, but this is the dilemma: the story of two mes. So to think I should completely forget one and wear the other would be a falsehood to myself. But it's okay to leave the gangsta on the shelf and be a gentleman at all times and try to stay on track because to tell you the truth it's nice not having to watch my back. But remember all the rules you learned as a gangsta and use them with the gentleman because if you forget you're a phony and a falsie and you migh' as well work for the Jakes but don't get crazy. One day at a time because a gentleman has to walk the fine line between the two but who knew there could be one of me and two of you.

KARMA / Faruq

I always found the concept of Karma intriguing. I was raised as a Christian, and converted to several different Islamic sects as an adult. I am now a confirmed spiritualist who believes in the beauty of all religions and great spiritual philosophies. As a teenager in the 1960s, I was attracted to all the countercultures my generation was participating in and discussing around the college campuses: Black Power meetings, civil disobedience protests, sit ins, walk outs, etc. We also discussed different religious, spiritual and other existential ideas—so popular then—at the parties where we always gathered after protests.

So Karma made sense to me at my earliest acquaintance.

At that early brush with the ancient philosophy, all I had was a very elementary understanding. However it helped me to make sense out of an insane world. All the blind hatred and injustices of racism, misogyny, colorism, nationalism, classism. All man's myriad discriminations and -isms. Karma basically said that what we do in life comes back to us: what we give, we get back.

As simple as my understanding was then, it motivated me in attempting to treat people fairly. However, my anger at injustice and my own lust, greed, ignorance and irresponsible behaviors distorted my decision-making abilities. I heard some but not all the messages expounded upon at those meetings because I was focusing, anticipating and prioritizing about the parties I knew would come after the meeting. It is sad to look back and see how prevalent this dilemma was among so many of my friends. It is one of the distinct reasons many historians give for the failures of the Sixties' movements. I was one of millions. But this is my memory.

So I missed too much of the methods. I thought you just showed up with your anger, quick wit, charm, raised fist and a confident assured nod of the head. I found out too late that service was the rent money that had to be paid to retain your chair at the table. I missed that part of the Karma. You have to give to get. Not just know about it and talk it good. Disciplined effort and the slow grinding work that went on while the parties were happening somewhere else was where you earned your good Karma.

At the parties, I was becoming an addict, a womanizer, and a manipulator. My Bad Karma was growing exponentially.

Much later, in prison, I took a fifteen-year course in Siddha Yoga and learned that Karma is so much more than I imagined when grappling with my meager understanding in the Sixties. Part of Siddha Yoga's theory of Karma explains how Karma stretches over many lifetimes.

One shortcoming of mine—if it can be considered a shortcoming—is I have never been able to believe every tenet of any belief system or religion I've ever practiced or studied. Karma comes closest for me to complete acceptance. I think it is because it helps me to believe I don't have to know the unknowable. Which came first, the chicken or the egg? Why did the Godly Serving Nun get killed by tyrants while trying to help the poor, while evil gun dealers lived out long lives of complete debauchery? Or why did the baby get run over by a drunk or die of incurable disease, never to have known any joy? My understanding of Karma has helped me to stop being eaten up inside believing I know what is fair and who is coming up short. It has taught me that I only need to pay the rent by serving justice. Serve the principles of the Great Spiritual traditions.

I still come up short too often but I've learned the merit of the effort. What's fair is always easily found if we just look in our hearts not our heads, our hearts where all truth exists.

WHAT I LOST / Khalifa

It would be hard for me to define what I lost when I was incarcerated, basically because I was lost from the start. Being raised in a culture that recognized and promoted a tough guy image or a fearful community respect of willing violence pretty much today reveals to me I was chasing the graveyard. So what I lost was an early burial if put in perspective.

I would have liked to say I lost out on an American education, but that wouldn't be truthful 'cause I was kicked out in the seventh-grade! I'd like to be able to lie and say I had all these promising lanes and support persons to cheer and aid me on, but again a fake ass vision of a black welfare family with Ozzie and Harriet dreams! This meal may be even more digestible if I said I was a "Manchild in The Promisedland"; at least that would provide a really close picture of the times, the poverty, the overflow of negative role models, and of course the number of juvenile homes including foster homes I was passed through from the age of nine till I was seventeen. But again, who really cares? Speaking from today's mindset, everything that had any meaning to me was "taken" from me! My identity, my love of life (as I knew it—regardless of your prescribed pictures) my innocence as a child and self-esteem and spirit to want to do the right things. But what's right in a marginal world that doesn't want you anyway? Quite frankly, I lost respect for storybook-tellin' mutherfuckers who had me believing somewhat that I could put an honest American life together no matter what, that second chances were a part of the foundation of this evil country which I live in, (well state for sure), what I lost is trust in a society that has no conception of, or willingness to forgive. Yeah, I lost respect for most teachers, and preachers, judges, and social workers, so-called friends as well alleged protectors, because I have found that they are mostly supporters of an unjust system and would rather go alone than to make serious corrective changes. But, I have found "Faith," and in it I find the balance that encourages me to not give up!

sometimes i
watch my breath
nd writes like i'm slap boxing with the
nd that nigga cheats, so i
nt that's how et is in a cell
n and all that I will e
nts of a cell.
veryday in this tragedy,
nings anything resembl
g well it turns into a tragic m

CHAPTER 2

RUPTURE

LOSSES / Khalifa

After the sentencing phase of my trial, I was lost!

In a fog of mental numbness, thoughts of confusion clouded and shattered all life's visions.

I really didn't know freedom to compare any further denials of it with, yet one of my strongest feelings was to survive: that was already a forced position in my life.

I was never in the habit of looking back. Pain and exploitation was constantly a challenge in front of me. "The rest of your natural life," bouncing off the walls of my brain! Who in the hell is this dude—we never even fought—sitting there like some want-to-be god or lord of some old-ass English estate? Did he just say that to me?

My life! (Laughter inside.) I knew from pain that I didn't have a life. If he knew anything about me, that much would have made him feel foolish. "Stand up!" (Two arms grasping mine, leading me away through a side door from the courtroom.) I couldn't fix my eyes on anything: everything seemed to blur on me. My legs were actually weak (stay-up Chuckie, don't stumble now), down a spiraling flight of stairs into a hall that felt cold, a different cold than I recognized. Voices coming from a crowded bullpen: "What's up, Chuckie?" "What they do?" "You alright?" "Be strong brother," but they merged in my head like a slowed-down record being played, and the numbness grew.

Being led back to the county jail, noise rising loudly from the circle, I vaguely heard someone say, "Diggs is back." A silver door opens. I'm ushered through. A finger points to the sergeant's desk, guiding me, and no one wanted to say anything, just stares. A friend taps me on the shoulder and says, "I heard you took it all. Man you different. Anything you need holler," and he turned to walk away. I stopped at the desk only to be asked, "Is everything alright?" I didn't even respond, I simply looked at the sergeant as if he was crazy. I may have nodded, and I headed to the tier. Tier Twenty-Three—everybody on the tier was there for homicide and watching me as I crossed the circle of the county jail.

As I entered the lower level of the block, a voice called out, "Chuckie, wait a minute." He ran over to me grabbed me by my arm and pressed a tin foil packet into my hand and said, "You know who this is from. If you need anything he said let him know . . . Hey, take it easy bro, everybody's looking at you." I kinda knew what the packet was, so I said, "good lookin'" and proceeded to climb the one flight of stairs to the tier.

Once on the range, my partner came over to me and just stood looking at me, I guess the news had reached the jail before my arrival, cause he didn't say a word: just stood there, then after what seemed like an hour reached out and put his hand on my shoulder and said, "You'll get 'em man, I know you won't give up." I opened my hand with the packet in it and said, "I'm gon' sit down." "How you feel," he said, "yeah, I'll go with you." We went to the back of the cell I was in and as he stood in the door watching for guards or others I opened the packet and looked up at him and said, "Man don't worry about none of that today. I ain't going for nothing, I have nothing to lose and nothing else to gain." I ran some water in a cap I used for an ash tray, and pulled my syringe from the hiding spot, put some powder in, pulling a little piece of cotton from a Kool filter, rolled it between my fingers and dropped it in the cap, I began to draw-up and my man said, "Be careful man, they said it's good." My look remained the same, and I filled half the syringe up and instinctively went to my pay-off vein, ran it in and withdrew, didn't boot or nothing, lit the remainder of the cigarette and told my partner, "Go ahead, it's on you."

Nodding, in a fog. Lost. Time stood still and I felt it was all happening outside of me. It just wasn't real. This ain't happening. Nobody takes my life without resistance, fuck that dude. He'll see I ain't done. And I faded into another nod. Lost!

SPACE / Khalifa

I wasn't sure how long I stood there, aware of the blurring sound of the loud speaker from the circle. I kept telling myself yesterday was just a bad dream, and so was last week, in fact as soon as the paperwork was straightened out they'd find the error and correct it. Yeah, that's what's happening. Life! It still hadn't registered in my mind. I just couldn't digest the sentence, the meaning or the audacity of that judge saying some shit like that to me.

A lot of cats I had listened to said that only meant like twenty years, saying if I kept to myself and avoided trouble I had a good chance of getting out! But damn, twenty years no matter how you looked at it was a long time, and just what was I supposed to do for twenty years? It wasn't going to change anything. And what needed to be changed anyway was "me." The truth is I was defending myself. Yeah, that's right. They don't know how it is on the streets. They don't care that several of their own people were some of whom I was buying drugs from and for sure they don't know how my life had been affected by all the too-far-to-reach ideals they had planted in my head about being good! Who was good? What is good! I know that being weak ain't gon' get you nothing but left alone! And who in the hell wants to be left alone? That is a feeling only people who have everything they think they need feel. It sure ain't a feeling of the invisible, people like me who had to announce themselves, otherwise people would come in and step on your feet. They'd sit on your lap saying they didn't see you sitting there. They'd talk and say things, mean things, hurting things, painful embarrassing things, things you would be punished about if you said them about them; but they acted like you weren't even there and talked about your clothes, your drinking father, your brother who's in prison, and how they always see you on the corner when you're supposed to be in school. They talk to make themselves feel so much better, cause they couldn't make it in your world.

Um hum, and they gon' give me a life sentence . . . "Hey Chuckie, come on up I got a wake-up."

I started down the spiraling set of metal stairway, passing several guys arguing about their cases, talking about what the police can do and can't—what's lawful and what's the difference in their entrapment and being set-up. I passed a shake-down on the lower tier, three guys were surrounding a soldier that had been brought to the county for being AWOL: they wanted his watch and he seemed reluctant to give it up. Finally, I reached the bottom and yelled out for the booth guard to hit the lower gate, which he did, once he looked down and saw who it was.

My man six-something was standing at the corner of the cellblock nodding to me. We went through this greeting handshake thing of prisoners; it was a special handshake with an unspoken commitment, a declaration of trust and camaraderie that pledged a dual kinship of life, fight and respect.

We went in through the bathhouse into the back where the barbershop was located, passed through the supply door and kinda closed the door behind us. We stood facing each other as he reached into his pocket and pulled out two fat joints, handing me one he said, "This some good shit bro. I just got it last night."

I lit the joint—took a long hit, and turned to peer out the door to ward off anyone approaching that wasn't a part of our tribe. Exhaling the smoke, and feeling the lighting of all my thoughts get small, I watched as brothers bumped each other going in and out of the doorway, I watched as they jockeyed for the barber chairs, getting ready for court appearances and possible window visits. I watched the muggers size up potential prey and mark them with simple eye movements to their crew. I watched and thought briefly about how this was going to be the greatest feat of my now life, every day, all day: watching out for the predators as well as defining space, with or without respect.

FROM THE BOTTOMLESS / Malakki

What is your name?
My name is Ralph Bolden but most who know me call me Malakki.

Where are you from?
Pittsburgh, PA.

What did you do to get into prison?
I was arrested in 1994 after I robbed a gun store and shot two of the men who worked there. One of the men died and the other survived but was severely wounded.

What is your sentence?
I am currently serving a sentence of life without parole for the homicide, plus an additional 30 to 60 years for the robbery and assault charges.

Did you graduate high school?
Yes.

What did you do after that?
I worked in a local amusement park, then I joined the Army. My job was to drive a tank. I served my three-year enlistment and received an honorable discharge.

What did you do after the military?
I worked various jobs until I got a pretty good job doing maintenance for the light company. I had a side job as a janitor and I began making money from my hobby as a DJ doing weddings and parties. I was trying to adjust to civilian life but I began having difficulties with depression and feelings of anxiety.

And the prejudiced treatment I had to deal with in the Army put a chip on my shoulder.

How was your relationship with your family at this time?
Everything was okay, but I know that my mother and little brother knew I was having problems.

Were you in a relationship or dating?
I had been in a few relationships until I met Juel. We fell deeply in love with one another and we got engaged.

Why did you do the crime you did?
It got so bad with me that I started having anxiety attacks and rebelled to where I quit working. I kept DJing here and there but things with me got worse and I ended up in a mental hospital for a couple of weeks. When I got out, I started hanging out in the streets with the wrong crowd and self-medicating with marijuana. Then things got hectic when gangs started popping up all throughout Pittsburgh. People from other neighborhoods started riding through and shooting at us. I bought a gun for protection.

      As my anger and anxiety worsened, I went to a gun store to rob it and get more weapons for the neighborhood so we could defend ourselves. I had never done an armed robbery and I got really nervous. The anxiety had me stressed out, so of course; I panicked. I wish I could go back and change things.

How did the police catch you after?
Someone from the neighborhood was a secret informant. When I showed up with the stolen guns, he contacted the police.

Where were you arrested?
I was arrested at my mother's house the day before Thanksgiving.

How did it feel when you knew you were going to prison?
At first, when all the officers came in pointing guns and yelling, I thought of how frightened my mother and little brother must be. Then my mind went blank and I got this terrible feeling in my stomach as they put the handcuffs on me. Then my hearing and vision seemed different as they took me out of the house and it seemed like I was watching a movie.

Were you scared going into jail?
There was some fear but because of the military and hanging out in the streets, I knew how to deal with fear and I wasn't afraid to stand up for myself when I got challenged by someone. But some of the things were very scary I saw happen to other people who didn't stand up for themselves.

What's it truly like to be in prison?
I lost everything when I was arrested. First, I lost my freedom. Then I lost my fiancée. Most of my family shunned me and even my mother had to adjust and find a way to deal with me and what I had done. I lost my home, my truck and all of my possessions. Then I lost every hope and dream I had ever had (getting married, having children, owning my own business, traveling, etc.). Then I lost God. So it turns out that after I killed someone, everything I ever loved died also. Now, imagine that state of mind teamed up with all of your regret and misery, and you're locked in a cell about the same size as an average bathroom for year after year facing execution. That's what it feels like.

How long were you on Death Row?
It took five years for me to petition the court and receive a life sentence.

What's it like knowing you'll spend the rest of your life in prison?
It hurts. It hurts bad. At first, it felt like my soul was dying a little bit every day and nothing I did made it better. I started feeling like a zombie trapped inside of a living grave. I'm doing better now and one reason is because I have gained remorse for those I've victimized and I accept the responsibility of my actions. Because of what I've done, they have suffered far more than I can imagine and knowing this defeats the shroud of self-pity I used to drown in. But on bad days, it's hard sometimes to keep the tombstones out of my eyes, especially when I'm surrounded by so many who have surrendered to the conditions and have become walking corpses. In time, I found a relationship with God that gave me better strength to endure the struggle and also gave me a hope that someday I will walk out of this prison and return home to my family.

If you could do one thing in your past differently, what would it be?
I would have listened to my ex-fiancée, Juel. I'm blessed to say that after many years we are friends again. Back then, she tried to help me and she asked me to stop hanging around negative people. She also encouraged me to take some college classes because back then, she saw something in me I didn't see. I'm sorry about the crime I did, but I'm more sorry that I didn't put my pride to the side and be honest about my anxiety, and then accept Juel's love and support as well as taking her advice. If I had done this, I would not have robbed that gun store and pulled the trigger and shot those men.

FIT TO KILL: A REACTIONARY EXISTENCE (PART ONE) / Malakki

My name is Ralph, but most call me Malakki. I am presently doing a prison sentence of natural life plus thirty to sixty years running consecutively. People often ask me what it feels like to serve a life sentence. The best way that I can describe it is that every day, I feel a piece of me die inside. It is a silent steady subtraction of a me that I used to be: a concept of myself that I easily held and comprehended that I now can no longer grasp.

After twenty years, it feels like I was born in prison, and have always been in prison. And it feels like all of my memories of a life prior to incarceration are just some shit I made up in my mind to seem relevant or a little more human.

When arrested, I went through various stages in regards to the crime I committed and my perception of it. At first, I lied and blamed some unknown assailant and totally denied any association with what took place. Next, I accepted my actions but blamed them on "the devil." I argued that it was the Prince of Darkness' enticement that led me to commit such a horrible act.

Then I finally accepted full responsibility and blamed it on the gravity of "the streets" that lulled me into an anti-social mode of being. But none of these excuses are adequate descriptions of what actually took place with me so many years ago. In my mind back then, I saw a greater good in a path that was paved with aggression, violence and, as my actions proved, death.

It is difficult, twenty years later, to offer any currency to the mindset of the confused and angry young man I used to be. No resonance exists between whatever motivated my youthful act and my older self. It's impossible to try to recapture. With that said, I know that my intentions even then were to bring something good from the destruction I caused. I wish I had someone I could have trusted, someone who I could have laid out my purpose to and who would have told me that there was a different way, a better way, not paved in blood.

It took time before I was able to have remorse for what I had done. At first, it was just wishing that I hadn't gotten caught. Then it was regret that I would have to serve the ultimate penalty. But in time, I began to experience a contrition that was unconnected to me or my feelings: sincere remorse was beginning to take place. I'm not where I should be as far as putting myself in the shoes of the victims, but I'm better than I used to be.

I say this because, without doubt, even if I had the perfect plan to do the robbery again—a way in which I couldn't possibly be caught—I wouldn't do it. And in this way, I would avoid shooting those two men.

I say this without fear of being considered "soft" or weak. In the past, even if I had felt like this, I would have never been brave enough to express it. But I know now that it is the strong one who is willing to face criticism for their point of view. And it is also the strong one who can control their impulses and the weak one who fails to scrutinize their whims and just simply follows their compulsion.

I wish I would have known things like this before I shot those two men in the robbery of a gun store, killing one of them. I wish I had a higher concept of how to be on the earth. But I didn't.

What you are about to read is my journey from war head to a peace of mind. If you are presently suffering from inner turmoil, trust me; it is better to not do something and feel like a loser or a coward, than to actually do it and become a loser and a coward for *not* standing up for the better part of yourself. I hope this gives you insight in regards to the severity of the consequences you could possibly face if you follow my footsteps. Please, think twice.

Prison is an American reality for people like me. Either we would end up inside of one, or a family member or friend would.

For us, prison is part of the human condition.

But there are those who would consider us less than human. From their point of view, how much humanity can exist in the heart of people who willfully break the law, especially for someone like me: a convicted killer? According to the media, especially the movies, prison life is filled with sub-human perverts who live a craven, bottom-feeding existence, continually stabbing, raping, and abusing one another, hungry for carnage and forcing others into submission.

When first led into a Pittsburgh jail, wrists squeezed in handcuffs behind me, I prepared myself to be offered at the altar of a nihilistic existence. Instead, I found in the old Allegheny County jail the same environment I had just left. The only thing different was the bars. After I was transferred out of intake, I was sent to the infamous "Murder Range," Tier 22, reserved for those accused of harsher crimes.

I noticed how cramped the cell was, about seven by five feet, with a fold-down cot, toilet, sink, and a small fold-out desk, then I took a walk down the tier. I saw men who I could probably click with, and others who I would avoid. I walked past three men who were looking for a fourth to play spades. I joined them. The only place there was to sit was on the floor. Other men had to walk around us and excuse themselves to get past.

Of the men I was playing cards with, the one who had the longest time in, Detroit, had been in county over a year waiting to be taken into Federal custody. The other two men had only been incarcerated a few months. In the middle of the game, the three men excused themselves and said that they would be back. I assumed that they were going to smoke or get high, but when they returned, there was no trace of any foreign substances.

We got locked in the cells for dinner and after they finished feeding us, the guards led us back out. We met up to play cards again and this time when the men asked to be excused, I sneakily followed. Detroit's cell was the closest, and when I peeped inside, which was a violation in all regards, I saw him standing with his arms folded across his chest. Then he said something in a low tone and bowed. Next, he stood up straight again, then went to the floor and put his head on the towel he used as a prayer rug.

After a couple of days of playing cards, going to meals together and talking, Detroit and I got cool. He invited me to the Islamic service of Jumah that Friday and I accepted. I spent the nights rewinding my mind back to the life I killed. Everything I was had died when I pulled that trigger, and it was hard to accept my social demise. As my mind traveled through my thoughts, I felt like a tortured spirit still trying to haunt my past life, too afraid or just unable to accept my present reality. I worked vigorously to ignore the loud pounding of my chiseling of my own tombstone. How can you still be alive when everything you were no longer exists? But there I was, like other ghosts in that prison, striving for existence.

The first visit I had with my mother was awkward. We sat in different rooms separated by a small, scratched window and I could only hear her comforting voice through a telephone line.

She said something like, "I don't want to hear about what's going on. Not right now. Just tell me what you need." I told her that I hadn't changed clothes in a couple of days and I needed underwear and socks, and a couple changes of clothes that I could wash and alternate until I went to trial. She talked about trying to find a way to get my one million dollar straight bail reduced, and I told her that probably wasn't going to happen. I asked about my little brother and my grandparents, who I knew were devastated about the news of me murdering someone.

As she talked, I thought about how many times I had ignored her feelings. All she wanted was for me to live a good life, and she did whatever she could to make that possible. I thought about how many times she had asked me to stop by and visit, even cooking for me when I said I would come, and then I'd get a phone call from a so-called friend and totally burn her. But where were those friends? I held out hope that some of them might show up or at least support my family. They never did.

The next visit came from my ex-fiancée a few days later. As soon as I saw her tear-soaked face staring back at me through the small, damaged window that separated us, I felt the heaviness of my own tears. She picked up the phone and as I put the receiver to my ear, she said, "How could you do this to us?" Her words scrambled my brain and I opened my mouth to respond but no words appeared. I thought, "What did she mean by 'us'? I'm the one in prison going through all of this; *me* not 'us'." Not sure what the subject actually was, I changed the subject and asked about her and her mother. I loved my fiancée, according to my definition and understanding of love, and I loved her mother so much that she was the only woman besides my own mother that I ever called "Ma." Of course, they were both hurt. She said, "How could you do this? It's like there's a side of you I don't know . . . it's like I don't know you."

That Friday, I attended the Islamic Service. The imam gave an arousing presentation that gave me the impression that he sincerely cared about all of us. The main theme was that we, as men, had a responsibility to not only our families but also to the greater community at large. He gave examples of his premise taken from the life of the Prophet Muhammad and verses he recited from the Qur'an. I was instantly impressed and saw his attempt to sway us away from criminality as part of a larger sphere.

What the imam said was basically the same message I had heard from people of different faiths or no faith in particular. All of these people shared space in the same focal continuum and despite how they offered examples of what they were trying to say, it all amounted to being good on the earth instead of bad.

But for some reason, the way the imam explained it reached me better than any other ways. I took to his message wholeheartedly and began to study Islam in the cell at night instead of replaying in my mind all of the mistakes and circumstances I had no ability to alter.

Detroit introduced me to his small circle of like-minded men, and they shared books and other material with me. I made the decision that, no matter what the outcome of the trial would be, I was going to be a better man. The material I absorbed at night gave me an impetus to correct my mode of being. But it was still jail, and I had a few altercations—some physical—mostly because there were so many men in such a small space. The number one thing that changed when there was a conflict was that unlike when I was still on the streets, where I had a circle of men who would cajole me into self-destructive behavior, I now had a circle that sought to keep me out of trouble and admonished me about my aggression.

Shortly after the fasting during the month of Ramadan, I received legal mail from the District Attorney's Office. I was standing on the range talking to someone while I opened it. I scanned through it and realized that the Commonwealth was seeking the death penalty. I made a statement like, "Look at this! These devils are just trying to scare me. There ain't no death penalty. That's some shit from the cowboy days."

An older gentleman who lived on the range and who had just happened to walk by stopped, came back to me, and said, "Young brother, you better take a look at that carefully 'cause they *do* still have a death penalty. I'd take that seriously if I was you." I said, "All right old head," and when he walked away, I waved my hand disrespectfully in his direction and said, "Ain't no God damn death penalty. They just trying to scare me." But I did go to the law library the next time they opened it up for our range. It was so cramped with limited space that it felt like being in the bottom of a slave ship, but instead of being surrounded by the creaky boards of the vessel we were encapsulated by piles of thick books. After two hours of reading and researching, I was more lost than when I started. Detrimentally, I decided to just use my wits and try to figure out my next step.

One day shortly after dinner, a guard came to the tier with a clipboard. He stood by the front gate and called a few names and mine was one of them. He explained that the new county jail was finished, and we were to be some of the first transfers because of the severity of our cases.

He said that after the final count, we would be called to the dining hall for a meeting that would explain the move procedure, and that we should bring all of our legal work to better process us.

After the final count, a guard came around and opened the cell gate. I started to just wear my shower shoes but he insisted I wear my boots. And I was just going to bring the paper that listed my charges, but he stressed that I bring every piece of legal work I had. Once in the dining hall, all of the guards came in and they locked the door. A captain told us that we were not returning to our cells and that we were being shipped out ASAP.

Groans and curses filled the room. We were forced to leave behind not only pictures that could not be replaced, religious books, letters, and addresses, we also lost every article of clothing and all the things we used to clean our bodies and take care of ourselves; everything.

They lined us up a few at a time, strip searched us, then we got dressed and shackled. As we hobbled out of the side door, we saw a large commuter bus—the same buses people ride to work in, here in Pittsburgh we call them PAT buses—that had a giant-size police light attached to the top of it. We piled in and were driven a few blocks to the new county jail. When we got there, we were herded out and inside we rode the elevator to the top floor in groups. Once on 8D, we were given a cell and stripped out and given a red uniform. Then we were given packages that had travel size bars of soap, deodorant, etc. We stayed locked in the cells for three days and only came out to eat on the new blocks. The new jail was drastically different than the old county jail; the cells were a lot bigger, there was central air, and the block had carpet.

Once they let us come out of the cells for day room, we realized that there was no outside yard, just a large room with an open gate that had a basketball hoop. I asked my mother for a Qur'an and a Bible and when she sent them, I read and studied with the other Muslims on the block. We began meeting together to pray and eventually the imam we met in the old county came to the block and held the Friday service.

After about five months, I was transferred down to the sixth floor where it was easier to go to the law library a couple of times a week. I tried again to understand what was going on, and I got better. Also, once I was sent downstairs, I knew more about Islam than anyone else on the pod so they nominated me to give the sermon on Fridays since the imam was only visiting upstairs.

I continued to get visits mostly from my mother and ex-fiancée, but it was like they were suffering from my situation more than I was.

It was over a year until I finally went to trial. I tried to remain tough and unemotional in court, but near the end of trial something happened. What helped me see things from a different point of view, which set me on the path to change, was what the wife of the man I murdered said in her victim impact statement at the trial. Although she was white, she reminded me a lot of my mother, and they probably had more similarities than differences. I didn't hear or feel an ounce of hate from her as she spoke; just pain for her loss. And, a kind of *pity* for me . . . it was like she was talking to someone who was void of any feelings or human compassion, and it was as if she felt sorry for me. (Again, this is how I perceived it.)

She explained to me and to the judge and the other people in the courtroom that I didn't murder just one person; this man was her husband but also her best friend, her children's father, someone's son, etc. As she spoke, the severity of what I had done became real to me. I felt my heart physically breaking because it was me who caused so much hurt and pain to this nice lady and her family. There were no justifications I could tell myself because the people I shot didn't do anything to hurt me or mine. Her husband just had something I wanted.

On a deeper note, after studying history, I now know that my past behavior was not only disrespectful of what my ancestors stood for, but that by choosing crime, I was part of the problem of what was happening in black communities.

It was hard for me to hold my composure. Back in the cell, the whole tough guy, hard-as-a-brick image broke down when the tears came.

I was found guilty of all counts and sentenced to death row. I was placed into solitary confinement and had to wait about three months in the county jail before I was sent to state prison. It was then that I began to suffer from what I call the "whys": "Why didn't God stop me?" "Why did God let all this happen?" And many more questions with no clear answers.

I was transferred to SCI-Camp Hill where they process inmates who transfer from county jails into the state system. I was put on AC (Administrative Custody) status, which is basically a fancy way of saying solitary confinement. I was sent to Camp Hill's RHU (Restricted Housing Unit or "the hole"), and it was the worst hole I have ever been in. Not only are the cells painfully small, the conditions and the treatment resembled what you might hear about in a third-world country.

As part of the classification process, they brought me

to this office one day while I was wearing an RHU jumpsuit, handcuffs, and shackles. I was given what I found out later were IQ tests. About a half hour after I returned to the cell, I saw guards forming around the cell door. They opened the cuff slot, and I stuck my hands through. When they had put the handcuffs on, they opened the door, pulled me out and pushed me up against the wall. Two of them patted me down like four times while a bunch of them tore apart the cell. Then the COs threatened me and said that if I had cheated on that test, there was going to be a problem.

I was totally confused because, not only did I not cheat, I had no idea what that weird test was for, anyway.

They took me back to the office and this time they gave me the test orally. They took me back to the cell, and about twenty minutes later, the staff member who tested me showed up in front of the cell door. That's when he explained what kind of test it was, and that I had done better than expected. I asked him how well I did, and he said that he couldn't go into detail but I should have been in a "university instead of a penitentiary."

WHY DID THEY GIVE UP ON ME? / Oscar

Why did they give up on me
and throw away the key?
Yes, mistakes were made
but change is at hand
turned from a boy to a man
trapped behind these walls,
I've seen many men fall
and succumb to death
but I've seen others never rest
until change comes.

Check your gun at the door
and join this war
of our minds
while we're here doing time.
Never waste a chance
to get hands
on this problem we have
that's getting bigger,
I'll do years if I pull this trigger.

Now
I'm walking it out wearing the browns
dressed the same like a clone
or better yet maybe a clown,
go and get my nose
the same color as a rose.
It's pretty funny
get my mirror
who's the dummy now?
Hear those doors close
nothing's funny now.

So get ready to
dance with the devil
in the pale moonlight;
you better learn to fight
or quickly run
because the war is on
'till death do us part
from the start
to the finish
it never ends
a lot of people are quick to pretend
that they can't be broken
but it happens daily.
The Commonwealth says,
"Fuck you, pay me!"
not with money, but time
I want all mine
if you get outta line
boy, I'll beat your behind.

Instead of
investing in change
they really don't care
so it's up to us to share
our thoughts and knowledge
in this convict college
where we're being watched
like hawks
trying to stop our show.
But it goes
on and on
and never ends—we're going to win
and see change
some day.

THE WORST DAY OF MY LIFE / Fly

Let me introduce you to the worst day of my life. This is the day my name turned into a number. I became inmate Martin aw8997.

The arrest took place at my parents' home. That was the address I used for any type of legal issues. On the morning of my arrest, my sister called and told me that the airport had called about a job that I had applied for through a temp agency. They said they would call back around 1:00 p.m. I got back to my parents' house around noon, and sat around anticipating the phone call. The phone rang, my mother answered and it was for me. Excited for the phone call and possibly a new career I rushed to the phone, just to be hung up on. The police were making sure I was home: at the same time, they were knocking on the front door and rushing through my back yard. They had a body warrant and a room warrant. After they searched the room, I was arrested and taken out the front door. All my neighbors watched in awe, because this was the first time that the police were ever at my parents' house. I was ashamed, I felt like I disgraced my family. Even though I was living a criminal lifestyle, I had been very careful about bringing any of my drama to my parents' home.

I was taken down to the Public Safety Building, which doubled as Police Station #1 in downtown Pittsburgh. I was taken to the Robbery/Homicide Division and interviewed by detectives Norman Leonard and Ferris Hutchinson. Norman was a very racist individual. He had a real nasty attitude and threatened me multiple times. The threats were minor compared to the beatings he gave me. His partner was no different. They're partners representing the law, but you would think they were partners in crime. He not only went with everything Norman said and did, but he backed him up with full force. This was at a time when getting beaten by the police was the norm, so I kind of expected this kind of treatment.

I was asked about a series of robberies that took place in the parking garages downtown. Their questions were more like statements. In their eyes, I was guilty of any crime they wanted me to be guilty of. I was interviewed for over four hours. The interview consisted of racial slurs, spit in the face, slaps, punches, and all other kinds of verbal, mental, psychological and physical punishment. I asked for my lawyer multiple times, hoping and praying that he would fend off this abuse. These police immediately replied that he was out of town. How they knew he was out of town was a mystery to me: I thought they were denying me contact with any outside sources so they could continue the abuse.

Come to find out, he actually was out of town. When I finally got in touch with him about a week later, he did not want to touch this case. I didn't understand why he wouldn't help me. He was my lawyer. He been there for me through my whole criminal career, until now I feel that these two detectives persuaded him to leave me hanging. How did these two detectives know my lawyer was out of town? There was only one way: they must have previously been in touch with him. These two were notorious for using force, money, or blackmail as persuasion tactics. My educated guess is that they got to my lawyer before I had a chance to.

After the interview, they charged me with five counts of robbery. From there I was taken downstairs to a cold, dingy cell holding cell, where I sat all day until my arraignment. My arraignment was not until 9:00 p.m. It was then my bond was set at $75,000 straight, meaning they wanted every red cent or I wasn't going nowhere but straight to jail. I guess that's where the word "straight" comes from: when they give you a straight bond. Go straight to jail, or for the lucky or more fortunate people straight home.

Since they charged me with five robberies, I knew my bond would be set high, but $75,000 in 1985 was unheard of. I had been thinking more in the range of $20-$25,000, with the chance of going through a bail bondsman, which meant only needing 10% of the money. Which is reasonable. Obviously, I didn't have $75,000 in my pocket. I didn't even have that kind of money at my disposal. So my mind was racing a thousand miles an hour and I was only trying to grasp at one thought. That was an impossible task: there were just too many. All the "what ifs" had to come to a halt. The damage was done. Now I had to come up with a new plan, and that was easier said than done.

At this point I was trying desperately to get in touch with my lawyer. That's when I was advised by his secretary that he was out of town. I had no time to waste and no time to wait: my next court date (my preliminary hearing) was in seven days.

David O'Hanissan, an Irish attorney in Pittsburgh, said that he would take my case. As I sat in my cell thinking about my upcoming preliminary hearing, a guard came to the cell, and told me that I was wanted up front, at what they call "the shoe." This was the part of the jail where they bring people in and take them out. I was confused, because I knew that I didn't make bond. When I got there, Detectives Leonard and Hutchinson were there. They seemed proud of themselves, with evil looks on their faces, like grim smirky half smiles. I knew this couldn't be good.

Leonard and Hutchinson cuffed me, took me back to the station for more questioning, and charged me with seven more robberies. Now, I was no angel, but all of these robberies did not have my stamp on them. One of these robberies included a sexual assault. Another one, someone was beaten real bad and put in the hospital. That definitely was not my MO.

From there, I had another arraignment for the new charges. This time, my bond was set at $100,000 straight. They wanted to make sure that my freedom was not a possible thing for me to attain, so I'm sitting in jail with a $175,000 straight bail: that sounds more like ransom money to me. Needless to say, I had no one to pay it for me.

I was going out of my mind at this time. I was basically a dumpster. What I mean by this is, I was getting high on anything that came my way. Which was only a temporary fix: once that high went away, reality was there waiting for me.

LIVING GRAVE / Malakki

To anyone who is reading this and is still focused on the "Street Life," I understand that the only person who can really change you is you. But do you really understand what can happen to you because of one bad decision? The crimes I committed took about five minutes, but in that short amount of time, I killed a man and severely injured another. I sent their families (as well as mine) on a long journey of heartache and suffering, and I will spend the rest of my life as a Lifer: one of the walking dead in a living cemetery.

Before I go any further, I would like to apologize. Not just to the people I hurt and their families, as well as my family, but I would also like to apologize for setting a bad example for my little brother and the other young people who witnessed my behavior. Ain't nothing cool about carrying guns around and being in "the game." I now understand that men are supposed to be the protectors of their communities. I apologize for being a destroyer. Nineteen years ago, when I was on the streets, I never bothered to question my actions or sincerely consider the repercussions of my behavior until the handcuffs cut into my wrists.

I hope that no one reading this will follow my footsteps and end up in prison. But if you choose this life, I want you to know a few things: number one, if you do dirt, you get dirt. There is no way around it. You can't get anything positive from living a negative life. At first, it seems like everything is going your way until Karma hits you right in the face. You'll see.

And when you become an inmate, you become a slave. Not a plantation slave, but the state owns you: you become state property. If you don't believe me, read the Thirteenth Amendment to the United States Constitution. Once you are "duly convicted" of a crime, you lose your freedoms as a citizen. One of the most important freedoms you lose that I hate that

I don't have any more is your right to privacy. You can't use the toilet in private. You can't take a shower in private. And worse than that, a guard (they are called correctional officers, or COs) has the authority to touch, search, and handle the little bit of property that you are allowed to have, and they also have the authority to pat search as well as strip search you.

If you have never been pat searched, you have probably seen one done in movies or on TV. Do you know what happens during a strip search? After almost two decades in prison, it is easy for me to explain.

First, they tell you to take off all of your clothes. Once you are totally naked, they tell you to stand up straight and open your mouth. They look in your mouth and tell you to raise your tongue. They look up your nose then tell you to turn your head and look to the right and fold back your left ear, then turn your head to the left and fold back your right ear.

Then they tell you to raise your arms, hands over your head, and they check your armpits. Next, they tell you to hold your arms out in front of you and they check them and tell you to show both sides of your hands.

They visually inspect your body, and if you have a stomach like I do, they tell you to lift it up and then they look in your navel. Next, they tell you to separate your penis from your scrotum and they inspect your private area. (I don't know what they do in regards to women prisoners, and I can't even imagine how horrible this must be for them to go through.)

Then they tell you to turn around and face the wall and they make you raise one foot at a time and wiggle your toes.

The last thing they do is to tell you to bend over and use both of your hands to spread open your butt cheeks. I've even had the COs shine a flashlight on my rectum as I bent over to further demoralize me for the sake of a "proper search".

If you choose the behavior that will give you the

consequences of prison, you will be forced to undergo periodic strip searches. Most notably, whenever you get a visit, you will be strip searched before *and* after you meet your visitors. My mother doesn't know this but I guess she will learn about this now if she reads this. I tried to keep this to myself for the past nineteen years and mask my humiliation, because she has been through enough drama because of me.

WHAT IS IT LIKE TO GET A LIFE SENTENCE? / Shawn

Coming to prison with a life sentence without parole at twenty-five years old is a feeling that I really cannot explain. I was angry, confused and upset that I put myself in this position. In the beginning it was very hard because this was not my first time in prison. I was a parole violator. I did three years the first time I came to prison, and I did not learn anything that first time. Even though I was out of prison for three years on parole, I did not stop doing crime. When I first came home from prison, crack was the new drug being sold in my neighborhood. At first, I tried to work, but my time in prison had taught me to dislike listening to someone tell me what to do. In prison, it was "do-what-I-tell-you-and-do-not-ask-questions", so I did not like taking orders when I was in the outside world.

Returning to prison, I kept getting into trouble not listening to the officers. I would receive misconduct after misconduct, and I spent my fair share of time in the Restricted Housing Unit (RHU or "the Hole"). After about two years of going in and out of the RHU, I had a counselor named Mrs. Chamberland who came to see me in the RHU to explain to me that I could not keep living my life like this. She mentioned the one person who meant the most to me and told me to think about her: my daughter, who was only two years old at the time. I came to prison while my daughter's mother was four months pregnant, so I have been in prison my daughter's entire life. Mrs. Chamberland and I talked about my daughter, and how I might get transferred far away from her if I did not stop getting in trouble; I made a promise to her that if she got me out of the RHU, I would change my life around. When I was let out of the RHU, I told myself that I would not get into any more trouble. But while Mrs. Chamberland was on vacation, the prison transferred me to SCI-Smithfield, two-and-a-half hours away from Pittsburgh. I was crushed, and the first thing I asked my new counselor at Smithfield was how could I get transferred back closer to home to be near my daughter? I was told that since I had a life sentence that I had to be misconduct-free for ten years. So I stopped hanging with my friends who were getting into trouble. I got me a prison job in the law library, and I stayed in my cell most of the time. I was blessed to get visits once a month, because my daughter's mother would catch a bus that came to the prison once a month. Because I was so far away from home, I stopped smoking weed: if you got caught smoking weed, the prison would take away your visits and I did not want my daughter's mother to travel all the way to see me and be told that she could not see me because I was in the RHU. I felt that she may not ever come to see me ever again.

At SCI-Smithfield I took a parenting class, and I became a peer educator of a program called Citizenship because my counselor asked me to. That was the beginning of me finding what I liked to do in prison: to help other inmates who were going home to not come back to prison in the same situation I was in with a life sentence. So over the ten years at SCI-Smithfield I was involved in being a peer educator of many groups, and it just became "my thing." I love being able to be someone that another person can come to for advice. I was lucky with my change because I learned early that there was something called commutation and I could work my way back to the outside world if I just stayed out of trouble and kept my "nose clean."

After my ten years at SCI-Smithfield, I was transferred back to SCI-Greensburg. After three years, SCI-Pittsburgh opened back up, and my counselor at SCI-Greensburg asked me if I wanted to go there. At first I told her "no" and she did the same thing that Mrs. Chamberland did; she brought up my daughter. Even though Greensburg was only about one hour from Pittsburgh, being at SCI-Pittsburgh I would only be fifteen minutes away from my daughter and her mother. So I agreed to come to SCI-Pittsburgh.

While here, I was picked to be a part of this thing called Inside/Out. For me, my transition of change was early in my sentence, because I always had hope that I would one day be home with my daughter. Now my daughter is twenty-one years old and I am still incarcerated, but I want her to see me as a better person than what I was. She does not know much about my past because I *hate* who I was back when I was twenty-five. Now I live to try and make my daughter proud of her daddy despite that I am in prison so being a part of this think tank and all the other things I do in prison, is what I want her to know about me. If it wasn't for my daughter, I really do not know if I would still be alive because she gave me a reason for living and to not give up hope.

I hope this is what you were looking for as you know that I am not very good with writing. I am a talker. (Smile.)

POLICE / Khalifa

We know your blue code will cause you to forfeit your human code!
We know your primary orders are not to protect us, but to constrain us
We know you will lie
We know half of you guys don't understand cultural differences
We know too, that you certainly don't believe in the same God
We know, he who profits from crime, commits a crime
We know you'll base your rightness on "doing a job"
We know many of you suffer from or hide prejudices of race, hence your hatred is released under the uniform of blue where you are protected
We also know that the maximum charge allowable begins with the officer's arrest and most of you identify with unruly whites but view the activity as violent behavior with people of color—thus you stress the harshest charge and the highest bonds
We also know that the labeling of minorities opens the door for discrimination and disenfranchisement
We know of the tale of two cities. What you don't know is it's under new construction, for better or worse

PULL IT BACK / Malakki

Don't you wish you could
realign your mind
and
rewind back time,
and return to a time
when you were more inclined to shine?
Right now,
let me remind your mind
to find the time to climb,
when you do this you'll find
that a life of crime is really blind.
When you see this
you'll see the reality of the fact,
and you won't do what I did:
pull the trigger
and beg to pull the bullet back.

I wish I could pull the bullet back,
pull it back,
And un-kill that man
and put my life back on track.

I'm trying to plant wisdom in your head like a farmer,
To help you cope and grow some hope, and save you from negative
karma.
I write these words to help, I want my words to be a healing,
But it seems like I'm talking to zombies with hearts like
abandoned buildings.
When we do dirt, we hurt ourselves, and our own communities
We wreck,

We are just like vampires trying to bite our own necks.
We are just like sharks born with our teeth in upside down,
In a feeding frenzy, we destroy ourselves every time we bite down.
We helped bury our neighborhoods, shoveling dirt in people's faces,
Now that we're incarcerated, tell me, how does that dirt taste?

As for me:
I wish I could pull the bullet back,
pull it back,
And un-kill that man
and put my life back on track.

I wish I could resurrect him,
and un-dissect him,
And go back to the day before
a bullet
injected and wrecked him.
I wish I could cheat time,
and go back before I did crime,
and repeat my lifeline
and choose a way that's divine.
I wish I could stop myself
with the gun still in my hand,
Before I pulled the trigger,
before the bullet lands.
But as I seek to dismantle the act that condemned me,
I hear other people planning to do what I did, so grimly.
They are deaf to my warnings, and dumb about the facts,
and blind to my daily struggle
to pull the bullet back.

I wish I could pull the bullet back,
pull it back,
And un-kill that man
and put my life back on track.

After almost 20 years, my hindsight is 20-20,
In less than 3 seconds, I destroyed plenty.
I took someone's life and his loved ones I hurt,
Destroying my life in the balance because I wanted to do dirt.
Also, everyone who loved me felt the backlash,
In less than 3 seconds, destruction *en masse*.
As the decades pass me by,
while laying in a lonely prison rack,
You'll find me everyday
wishing,
praying,
dying,
to pull the bullet back.

s lea

ls of

ds of t

. And

visions,

you

implanted in

nny — long before

s, cause I know what we

of forgiveness, I envision

we'll progressively move forward

extend the hand of apology and corre

whom we owe a start such as

d Thurman(s), the Honorabl

of course the memo

evening bless

crafts

ves and fan

priority ca

to increase

schools and bu

convinced

safety of y

want to dis

as to talk about

legalized

ple of god

and the primitive

cause they plan

ght out have bee

application remains

but theres

some mention

media

Listen

well?

earnings of those w endure

human advancement

watching for

ick to murde

or jim c

ack of

themselves. And here

that actually punishes po

about accountability! The one

y concerned as to when your goin

to result in any

bullshit bec

yesterday

fire a

about it —

CHAPTER 3
LIVING IN PRISON

I'LL NEVER SWALLOW THIS PILL / Oscar

I will never throw in the towel and be consumed by this incarceration. I told myself that if I get convicted they can have my body but never my mind or spirit. To be broke in spirit or mentally is to be the walking dead. The joy and hope of a better future is enough to keep me going. As the old saying goes misery loves company and believe me there is a lot of that going on inside these walls. To lose your sense of humor is a major defeat within one's self. To completely abandon any sense of what was instilled in you by your parents or what wisdom you gained on the street and completely become a mental robot and wear some mask every day the LWOP (Life Without Parole) has won.

In the warrior spirit of Geronimo, or Toussaint, or whoever, I fight every day when I wake up to not conform mentally to some program. Maintain your spirit. Maintain your hope. Walk with pride. If one gives in to the severe and dangerous effects of institutionalization, they are the walking dead. So what I'm in here for whatever for however if the "hat fits let him wear it" and check this out—mine doesn't fit, period. At one point I thought I could sleep my time away if I just could get a prescription, and I did. Believe me they are quick to sedate you if you want. And then I woke up and said fuck that. To be a slave to some pill is the same as giving in mentally. So I shocked back and came to myself and said I'll do this on the muscle and get it how I live. I'll wake up every day and put my mental armor on and keep it moving. I'm not gonna pretend that it doesn't hurt being away from my family and thinking that I should be somewhere married with children, chillin'. But if I can remain in control mentally and sound in spirit, there is no way I can fear it. Meaning this incarceration. Never one to play the victim, I try to keep it real with myself. The food sucks. The healthcare sucks. It gets hot in the summer and cold in the winter. It's implied. Keep it moving soldier. Don't let the walking dead consume you. Get out of the misery circuit and come back to the land of the living.

To turn thirty in life, I never thought I'd see it. To know so many who have been killed, gunned down, OD'd, I count it a blessing to still breathe. I got ties all over this city from Lincoln Avenue to Homewood to McKeesport and Penn Hills, and when I call guess what people are doing? The same old stuff they were doing ten years ago when I left. So call the journey that I'm on what you want, I believe I need to be on it because there is no way I would have the insight or introspection within myself if this had not happened. I would be another statistic, a dead one that is. So I'll never swallow this pill.

FARE ENOUGH / Malakki

A life sentence in the state of Pennsylvania means a social death. This is the punishment that has been legislated by our state. Because we are guilty of taking the life of another, we lost the right to have a social life. But we still live. We breathe and love and hate and have okay days and better days, like all other humans. My questions are: Is life without parole enough of a punishment? And should there be a more just sentence?

Life without parole seems like a less barbaric sentence than the death penalty. But after the cameras leave, the judges and lawyers prepare for their next cases while the wheels of justice more forward, what has actually been accomplished? The family and friends of the victim have an empty place in their lives that a trial may not fill. And it is like the one found guilty is sent to the moon with limited provisions, leaving the tears of his friends and loved ones in his wake.

Now there is one thing that I want you to consider: the power of human endurance.

The victim's loved ones all must carve a new meaning of life from what's left behind. Although some don't, many do. They go on and decide to not let the perpetrator win. Many times, physical death of one causes the emotional death of others, and those who stand strong in defense of their dignity should be commended.

But we, the doomed, also endure. Some of us accept the call of darkness and flash and tumble into the jaws of oblivion. Some of us lose the few pieces of us that still kept us loosely defined as part of humanity, becoming the ultimate human hyenas. But others fight back. We use the meager scraps of self-determination we can scrape together in this abyss and are able to sew together shreds of dignity we inflate with hints of hope and use them to float above the depths of the living dead. We also should be commended.

It is my opinion that only those on both sides of the coin who chose to better themselves despite their situation or condition are in the best position to help others going through similar circumstances. People who suffered victimization and overcame their struggle are the best fit to convince someone grieving to find the inner strength to endure. And it is those who have caused pain and suffering in the past and who overcame *our* struggle also who are best equipped to find an answer to reduce the mindset in some individuals that says, "I am entitled to your possessions, your body, your *life* more than you. And because I'm stronger or more cunning, I deserve it."

Is life without parole enough of a punishment? Should there be a more just sentence? What if it was placed upon the shoulders of the condemned the duty to retroactively abort what caused the kill. And then they were given the support to continue to quash any hints of thought embedded in them that made it possible to steal another's life?

Once they offered plausible answers and actions in their present environments, shouldn't they be persuaded to share their conclusions with victim's advocates and others, but especially in face-to-face encounters with those whose actions are pushing them to the same empty destiny?

Prison as it is structured today offers the incarcerated no incentive to change our hearts. And this is especially true in regards to Lifers. As long as we go where we are supposed to go when we are supposed to be there, and don't intimidate any staff, we will be considered model inmates.

Meanwhile, there is not an adequate counseling or support system specifically designed for those who are never, ever leaving prison. Why should *anyone* change their heart? Doing time is much easier when you don't think about the actions that brought you to prison. It's much easier to tune out, shut down, and surrender to the impetus of the whim that caused your circumstance. For many, easy wins.

But I say fuck that. I tried easy and it led to severe consequences. I've learned that following wisdom is much better than being a damn fool. But I am the type of person who doesn't use God to be good, or the excuse of a devil to act like a nut. It's *my* decisions, inevitably, that rule my actions. And since thought precedes actions, and actions inevitably dictate how I am judged and perceived on earth, if my worldview changes then how I am in the world changes. I get it.

I haven't changed who I am as a person but my mind set changed in how I see myself with all of my strengths and weaknesses. I'm not religious but I don't lie and do other vices because what you do, you become.

The myth is that only bad people come to prison. It is not for me to make this judgment but my family and loved ones will insist that I'm not a bad person. So what happened? The truth of the matter is that sometimes good people make bad decisions and even do bad things. This doesn't make it any easier for victims or their families, but it's the truth.

It was wrong for me to take another's life, and I deserve to suffer a social death for my actions. But what if I can stop the same anti-social, venal, monster that enticed me to a bad decision from possessing someone else? Shouldn't part of my sentence be to stand in defense against what I've done and act against it ever happening again?

The inmates I mentor here have already committed crimes, and my goal is to prevent more damage to our social structure once they leave. But what if people like me served as "medics" to the lost and dispossessed *before* another hospital visit or funeral? Think about it.

Especially think about it when someone you know or heard of is victimized by that man or woman that *everybody* knows is trouble. 9-1-1 doesn't seem to help. But maybe a one-on-one from someone like me might. Or are you just going to continue to do nothing and assume that handcuffs cure criminal hearts and let the violent, greedy, and pushy cycle their way to someone like me? But what if that someone doesn't have a positive agenda, only a damage plan?

It is up to people like me to make them better criminals or better citizens once they get to prison. Even if they attend programs for a couple of hours, I live beside them. We share the same eating utensils, same showers, toilets, and sleep in spaces more intimately close than perfect strangers in a Western society are used to.

And in my present condition, more incentive lies in putting batteries in their backs and releasing them upon the community, fit to kill.

But I say fuck that. I have many reasons for my decision to be a better person. But if I had no other reason it would be to prove the state wrong. Since I no longer choose to be a violent criminal, I am worthy to share the same air with you, and I will prove it by my actions of activism and the patient care I offer to the condemned and the dispossessed.

And my only incentive is the price awarded for honing a higher discipline: fare enough in the bowels of hell, surrounded by war heads, to have a peace of mind.

I offer my condolences to the victims and their families.

IN A CELL / Malakki

In this cell,
I'm giving fair ones to all my demons,
and every nightmare wakes up to worse dreaming,
but that's just life in a cell.

Months without mail
makes days slow as a mile to a snail,
I try to smile to prevail,
while inside I
feel more foul than sheets in a cheap motel,
and sometimes only a growl can stop the fail,
but that's just life in a cell.

Sometimes it's like it's hard to really
catch my breath,
and it's like I'm slap boxing with the Angel of Death,
and that nigga cheats, so I'm looking for a ref,
but that's how it is in a cell.

Coping,
everyday in this tragedy,
hoping,
I won't turn into a tragic me.
Prison has its own gravity,
every year it increases its potency.
As it changes me, I fight to remain some of the me
that I used to be
but that's RIP in this prison's hell.

I watch many come to prison
because they terrorize,

all through their lives
they watch their errors rise.
But once in a cell
they find out their mirror lies,
as they watch tears drip and rip
from clearer eyes.
But that's just life in a cell.

Too many of us wanna be gangsta
and we talk too much,
on the streets with the heat
we plot too much.
End up in prison,
got caught too much,
or early to the grave,
got shot too much.
But that's life
in our hoods:
as it manufactures inmates
like a factory,
and gets us perfectly ready for
the cell therapy
of living in a cell.

It's hard to answer the question,
"What was in my head?"
What made me pull the trigger,
and make somebody else dead?
What was the thing that
died inside of me,
that made me kill another
and start this insanity?
It started with arrested development

that led to an incarcerated mind,
within a neighborhood prison factory
that paved my way to a physical cell.
But that's just the kind of things you recognize
after a con wrecks then lets cognition rise,
and you reckon and then realize with
real eyes, when you're doing life in a cell.

Every regret gets re-visited
one thousand times,
and everything you wished you *didn't* say
gets un-said and you create new lifelines.
And everything you wish you *did* say
gets immaculately designed,
but this all happens in your God-damned mind.
And all it is,
is the time doing you,
instead of you doing the time,
but sometimes that's just your life
when you're living in a cell.

I wish I could find a way to
release me,
if not physically,
at least set my mind free.
But instead, I'll just
go make a chee-chee,
and try to find something half decent
on the TV.
But after the credits,
and my stomach's full because I fed it,
I'm back to trying to forget,
But then I forgot what I forgot to forget in the first place!

And that happens when living life in the worst place,
Confined in your mind while confined in a cell.

I wish I could
erase the erasing of my years,
because now that I'm sitting here it's clear,
that my criminal choice
was like listening to peer pressure
from a suicide circle's voice.
And my tragic actions
were like self-mutilating my social self
until I received the attraction
of death's satisfaction.
And as my soul succumbs
it's like my mind stays numb;
because it refuses to let me see,
that I should have let go of people
and hopes and dreams
that have *long ago* let go of me.
But that can't happen because
in that release,
every piece
of a fragmented peace
that I managed to lease
would greatly decrease.
And when the illusion dies,
the only conclusion alive
is that my closest thing to truth
is my most ardent lie.
And the only thing behind my eyes
is a me I no longer recognize.
But that's what happens
when you spend more time than you

care to consider,
living in a cell.

It gets to where
I can no longer fake it,
and don't care if I make it.
Everyday exposing staff,
like getting naked
for a strip and search,
and watching them become more afraid
that if White Jesus actually did go to
a ghetto-black church.
I'm sick of watching my decisions clowned,
and tired of hiding my pride in the
back pocket of my prison browns.
And I will keep my fake smile
turned up-side down,
because I realized the reality that
to the DOC,
all I am and all that I will ever be,
is the contents of a cell.

The cell kills anything resembling
a loving relationship,
it chokes them until they fail
and makes people jump ship and bail.
The cell kills anything resembling
real friendship or *true* kinship,
because it only survives through J-pay slips
and holiday mail.
So just to spite this
is why I write this,
it's against reality that I rebel,

so when the gate opens, my task
is to adjust my mask
before I leave the place I
say I hate,
but how can that be true,
when I finish what I do,
it's the place that I quickly rush back to:
this cell.

THE DISTINGUISHER BETWEEN TRUTH AND FALSEHOOD–ONE OF ALLAH'S 99 ATTRIBUTES / Faruq

When I came to prison, many of the guys I knew there had converted to Islam. As a twenty-five-year-old, still young and impressionable, I wanted to fit in, leading me to also consider converting. With my friends' encouragement, I went to Juma services. As faith or coincidence would have, the outside volunteer iman was from my community of Homewood, a district of Pittsburgh. The iman's name was Muhammad Ali and he had a small mosque around the corner from my maternal grandmother's house. As children, my brothers and sister spent many holidays and weekends at this house. My Aunt Geraldine and Uncle Big Otis also lived there. My most favored memories are of the time we had at that house.

Muhammad was the typical kindly cleric, kind, compassionate, humorous—always with a smile. He knew my whole family and seemed to have been almost waiting for me. Muhammad and several other older brothers whom I admired, eventually brought Mento (my rap partner) and myself into the fold.

In hindsight, when I took my vows to become a Muslim it was more a commitment to being a serious adult than to any surety of religious doctrine. At the time of my vows, I had not even finished reading the Qur'an, much less studied it. I was joining the brotherhood committed to being strong honorable men. Disillusionment with some concepts was to come later, with more introspection, experiences and more learned understanding.

Two new initiates and myself were given a list of Allah's 99 attributes, and instructed to choose attributes and we would attempt to emulate. I decided on "Faruq" for two reasons. First, in my spirit, if not yet in my actions, I was hungry to learn and grow, and distinguishing between truth and falsehood seemed inseparable from those tasks. Also "Robert" always seemed so common a name. "Robert," "Robbie," "Bob," "Bobby"—there seemed to be millions. "Faruq" had a unique sound and from my limited knowledge of Islamic names sounded uncommon.

I have consciously strived to honor the name, succeeding at times, and missing the mark at other times. Yet the name gave me a measuring stick that has been exceedingly useful.

So I remain Faruq.

TEACHING FOR THE UNIVERSITY / Faruq

Dr. Pugliano approached me with his usual demeanor. His pleasant smile, a ready chuckle in his big belly, an engaging tone of voice, comfortable with its intellect and sounding like it came from a fair intent. However this day, the usual twinkle in his eyes concealed a more serious intent. He wanted to talk business: the business of the University of Pittsburgh's prison education program, which he directed.

I had just gained an associate's degree from Allegheny Community College in Engineering Technology. I was also an undergrad in Pitt's computer programming department. Through my studies I had developed an affinity for mathematics.

Mathematics is often referred to as the exact science. Studying math, I could get lost for days finding the exact answer. That answer with no ambiguity, no colors, just the right number. Math was my way to step out of life's emotions and humanity's attempts of determining right and wrong based on cultural, social, religious and economic norms. No equivocation, just the correct answer! I found it exhilarating that the correct answer was always verifiable every time, everywhere in every language. A few years in on a life sentence, I could not find solutions for or correct answers to the hows and whys of my life's predicament. But if I worked at math with persistence, I could find the correct solution and prove its correctness.

The late nights studying. Falling asleep with unsolved equation notes on my chest and awakening with the correct solution jumping out of my dream: that was my own personal haven. Prior to college in prison, the only studying I had done was short cuts, gaming and playing. So when college, and math in particular, began creating these new insights and behaviors, I marveled at my new self.

Those early years in prison were like living in an evil

dark gladiator school full of crazy characters with a maddening mentality full of violence, drugs, deceit and sudden danger. My own mind was equally a dangerous place. Mathematics began to push back the dark corners. Systems of order, finding equity with several variables, discovering the area under a curve, not just playing it to the bust and hoping for the best, as my street self did: with mathematics I could make the crooked line straight.

I kept my studying to the schoolhouse and my cell, retaining my cool persona for my prison world. But now Dr. Pugliano was asking if I would be a student professor, teaching algebra and trigonometry for the university's accredited prison program and helping my fellow prisoners gain college degrees. I could hardly think, but I remember pride followed by dread. The pride was hearing that the professors from Pitt's math department believed I was qualified. Dr. Pugliano explained he would write out the curriculum for my first class, but my teaching technique and future curriculums would be up to me. He would only stop in occasionally to check my work and offer assistance. But dread gripped my stomach into knots. Could I really teach? Would students really listen? What would happen to my playya persona, my "I'll kill ya if ya cross me" image? Who was I now? Professor Bob? Would I try to be both? Up until that time I'd always boasted of being "the man of a thousand faces." So sure. Yeah. Play on Playya.

But learning and studying can become insatiable. I came to understand the maxim "we become what we do." Teaching gave me a sense of purpose and direction, not some ego trip of trying to control others' impressions of me. I found a comfort and sense of self-respect in teaching others a discipline my teachers had so graciously taught me. Teaching turned out to be honest and honorable. The more I strived to teach the more I learned. The more I learned the greater my need to learn. Teaching would not let me continue to keep playing and gaming. I was becoming what I was doing, teaching and becoming a teacher.

I went on to teach algebra and trig for the next seventeen years. It gave me so much, and when it ended it took so much. I'll write and tell ya about it sometime.

LOST AND GAIN / Faruq

The morning of November 9, 1993, started out like every other morning over the last forty years. That morning I woke up in an eight-foot-long, five-foot-wide, ten-foot-high prison cell. The cell contains a six-and-a-half by two-and-a-half foot bed, a three by one-and-a-quarter foot desk, a toilet, and a sink. These are the smallest cells in the country. The cruel joke is they are the size of coffins.

Prison has a slow moving, monotonous motion. The bland empty expressions the routine sameness, the empty hunger eyes intensely craving a taste of something undefined and just out of reach, the stumbling gait of listless bodies staggering through the crowded prison corridors has a Hollywood zombie movie quality. These zombies exist on the edge of existence almost motionless until the sudden movement of real life, a visit, an "I love you" over the phone, the telling of an old story, awakens the craving for a taste of real life again.

I have lived in one of these small coffin cells for thirty of the last forty years. The other ten, I've lived in what is euphemistically called a "big cell." What makes it a big cell is an extra three feet of width and a bunk bed. Approximately five of those ten years, I could stretch out in my "big cell" alone. The other three years were the hardest, when I shared my big cell and my miseries with another suffering man. We described it as "living in a bathroom with another grown-ass man."

I had risen early as usual and completed my morning rituals. These rituals I had slowly incorporated into a daily routine over the prior two years. I started developing these routines after I had finally quit using all mind-altering substances: a herculean task for me to say the very least.

I was intent on building a relationship with my higher power as suggested by the Narcotics Anonymous program and my NA sponsor. A famous NA tenet states, "If you ain't praying, you ain't staying." I wanted desperately to stay. I was past being sick and tired of being sick and tired. These rituals of mine consist of some yoga poses and breathing exercises, half an hour of meditation, and some daily spiritual readings. I needed these rituals that fateful morning, and many mornings after, for change, self-love and respect to remain my continuous goals.

I choose to believe it was the grace of what is holy and divine in the cosmos and beyond that prepared me for the heart wrenching experience on the morning of November 9, 1993. But what do I really know about why the world turns as it does? I can't claim the mantel of a great theologian or philosopher. I have tried to learn the secrets and songs of my own spirit. But hey, I could be tone deaf. At that point in my life I was just beginning to recognize the right notes to improvise on in my own song. God's dictates and choices are still way out of my realm of certainty. Maybe it's like Mom always said: "Robbie, you know God always looks after fools and babies."

I started getting high at thirteen—why we call it "high" is a mystery to me now—it was eventually the bane of my existence. It kept me acting like a baby, doing whatever I pleased, acting irresponsibly, selfishly believing the world existed for my pleasure alone. When such behavior exploded my life again and again, like a baby and a fool, I expected the world to answer my cries and demands. I would have carried the shame of those behaviors to my grave but Mom's lessons and NA's insistence on searching out my higher power had taught me how to forgive myself and others especially if healing and growing are my life goals. So whatever that power is, whatever name we agreed upon or choose on our own to call it, my God, just as Mom said, had truly granted me grace by helping me develop the strength I would need that morning.

Here I was, planted in the six-inch space between the end

of the bed and the sink. To navigate that space, I have to lay on my back, curl my legs into my chest, roll my six-foot, two-hundred-pound body, twist my ankles just right while flipping into a standing position between bed and sink. It's very difficult to stand in so small a space, bending over washing in a fifteen-inch sink sitting out from the wall groin high. It takes some practice not to splash water on the bed, floor, the TV next to the sink, pants, everywhere.

As usual, before I rolled into the wash up spot I had turned on the TV to the morning news. With soap in my eyes, I heard the news broadcaster mention my last name. I peeked at the TV screen trying not to get soap in my eyes and saw film of paramedics, and a mention of author John Edgar Wideman, my oldest brother. Hearing John's name in the news was not a big surprise anymore in 1993. I had heard the name many times in the media by then. But I thought I heard the newscaster say, "Noted author John Edgar Wideman's nephew has been found dead. Shot dead in a house on Flowers Avenue in the Hazelwood section of Pittsburgh." I looked at the screen and saw paramedics carrying a black body bag out of a house. My mind could not digest the information. The announcer spoke again, but my mind was shutting down rejecting the obvious. John's only brother with a son was me. But my son couldn't be dead. He was accepted to a college. He was turning his life around, too. He was my son. OH MY GOD! PLEASE! NO! Not my son. Not Omar.

I sat in shock for a few minutes, knowing what I had seen and heard. Yet a measure of disbelief, which I am sure was God's grace, pulled me through without a total breakdown until breakfast was called.

There is a surreal quality to losing beloved family members in prison, which is a difficult psychological negotiation. I cannot affirmatively claim it is less or more difficult than for people in other situations because I have been in prison for the deaths of all of my deceased family members since I have been an adult.

In prison, you cannot go through the process of gathering with relatives and friends to share grief, remembrances and accepting condolences. Sharing a meal, telling the old stories, crying, laughing and sometimes crying and laughing at the same time, emptying out and filling up. Mourning your loss while celebrating the one passed. In prison you just keep going on with your normal routine keeping up a veneer of normalcy thanking friends for their awkward attempts of condolences, claiming to be "awright" while pain and anguish explode inside your heart and mind.

The bell for breakfast rang, and I headed for the chow hall. I ran into a friend who asked had I seen the news and were they referring to someone in my family about the guy who had gotten murdered in Hazelwood. His words began a trembling, shattering emotional acceptance of the truth my rational mind already knew but my heart's mind was trying to believe away. It was as if I could make it not real if I just went about my usual routine and not think about it, some way it would go away.

I left chow without finishing my meal and ran for the phone.

I called my mother and the moaning exasperation that I knew so well in her voice finally made the tears break as I doubled over with the pain of this terrible impossible truth. My son, my baby boy, had been murdered. Taken away. Gone.

Mom's cry was so familiar: "Oh Robbie, it's Omar. They killed him." It wasn't the whole phrase that rang in my ears and tore at my heart. It was the "Oh Robbie" part. I had heard it a thousand times in my life. I had caused Mom so much pain. It had become engraved in the lines of her face, the slump of her shoulders and the enduring weight of her burden when she cried "Oh Robbie." It spoke volumes of love and disappointment. It echoed, "When will you ever learn, my beloved son." Now the greatest joy I had given her had also turned to pain and anguish. I heard so many things in her voice, but the most overwhelming emotion was responsibility and blame. I heard an old familiar refrain, "Oh Robbie, what have you done?!"

I am beyond certain Mom did not mean it that way. Her cry was for me, not at me. She cried for me losing my son and for her losing her grandson. Yet my aching soul heard her admonishing me about carelessly misplacing what's precious, and my old tired poet psyche heard, "When you don't pay proper attention you drop things and you lose stuff."

Even though I was sure my mother did not feel that way or cast those aspersions upon my hurting soul. I knew I felt it, and she knew me better than I knew myself. She always did. Yet her love was so encompassing. So somewhere in our pain on that cursed day, "When will he ever learn?!" screamed out at us both.

It was time to change, to stop the lip service, to stop the "I knows" and do something to create concrete change, not elaborate rationales. My inner self, my soul, my spirit, Jesus, Allah, Buddha, the Tao, the Shakti, what all religions and spiritual thesis have professed all welled up within me, the names, the concepts, screamed in unison through Mom's anguish and my hearts tears. "How did you let this happen?!"

Later I would see things more clearly and rationally. But at the time and in the succeeding days something broke, not just my heart. A degree of my overwhelming selfishness and self-centeredness broke. I finally knew I could change, and I would.

Inmates today can attend funerals of their immediate family members if their families are willing to pay county sheriffs to escort them—except Lifers. However, in 1993 Lifers still retained that privilege. Our families could pay to have us come view the body at the funeral home. Neither the family nor the prisoner could know the exact date or time the prisoner would arrive, presumably to prevent any escape attempts.

The next day, I was escorted in chains and shackles to the funeral home to view the body of my son, Omar Lateef Wideman. As the sheriffs turned into the Homewood section of Pittsburgh, my family's third-generational home, my heart sunk even more. The neighborhood had deteriorated considerably since I'd last seen it in November 1975. The streets were dirtier, the porches were leaning, lawns unkempt, house paint chipped, windows broken and boarded, many houses abandoned. Again, the feeling of responsibility: my conscience pointed its finger and hollered, "How did you let this happen?"

The power of providence, being ever the instructor, awaited me at the funeral home. Just as the sheriff's car pulled up, my ex-father in-law Gerald West was coming out of the funeral home. I loved Mr. and Mrs. West like they were my own parents. Mr. West saw the car, looked in, and our eyes locked. He knew just what to do. He ran in and got Mrs. West. From there, the word was out. Phone calls made, people saw each other at traffic stops, at the local market. Within minutes, friends and family from all over Homewood almost magically arrived at the funeral home.

The city police, who had taken me to the funeral home, obviously felt the positive spirit that had brought us all there without any preplanned or advanced knowledge and let everyone stay despite their rules that disallowed anyone being at the funeral home while I was there. I believe the highest power deemed it so, and so it was. So the two officers removed the handcuffs, leaving me in leg shackles and trusting the moment. The officers stood in the back of the chapel area with my brother John as he assured them there would be no trouble. My sister Letisha, who had also suffered the loss of a child, came and stood next to me at my son's casket. She held my hand and we cried silent tears. My sister and I have always had an inexplicable spiritual connection. We have always been able to ascertain when we need to get in touch with each other or when either of us are in crisis. It is almost like she can silently call me and I know to get in touch with her. I never feel the crisis or have any sense of doom or gloom. Some instinct just whispers, "Call Sis." As strange as it seems, this instinct has always existed between us.

So when she came and stood next to me at my son's open casket, we just held hands and let the tears run down our faces. Everyone else got quiet, knowing the sacredness of the moment and shared it with us in silence.

In that moment of pain, Geraldine, Omar's mother, came to my mind. I looked back and saw her leaning on the doorframe in the back of the chapel. It seemed the weight of this moment was so heavy she could hardly stand. I looked in her eyes, and for a moment could not see past her pain. Omar was the second son she had lost in less than two years. Her pain was beyond words. Yet she is such a great woman and a favorite of God. She was able to give me a moment. Her eyes let me in and showed me love and connectedness. She had been justifiably angry with me. I had broken her heart and abandoned her and Omar many years ago. Now our son lay dead, and I believed my abandonment played a part. But Geraldine, like my mother, is a great woman and at that moment only reached out to give me love. In retrospect, it only increased my pain and my love for and understanding of them and God's grace. Geraldine and I fell in love as children and despite life's twists and turns, the purity and sweetness of that love has always been our blessing.

I believe that all those present that day felt God's grace and power to deliver us blessed love in that time of pain and anguish. Not knowing what would be next or understanding how we had gotten to this place, we all recognized the completion and blessing of us being together in that infinite moment.

Remember, this was 1993. Gang war activity was roaring to new heights. The War on Drugs was in full swing, and America was building new prisons for young black boys and men captured and suffering under what, twenty years later, noted author and educator Michelle Alexander would aptly name "The New Jim Crow." Now my son Omar was a third-generation causality. My father, my uncle, myself, my nephew, now my son. All casualties of America's greatest sin—the self-perpetuating, hatred and ignorance-fed, blaming and finger-pointing racial oppression.

Back in my coffin cell for weeks without end, all I could think about was what could I do. I was a forty-two-year-old black man, an addict in recovery, a criminal, a Lifer with seventeen years already in prison, a new college graduate, a new math professor, a husband to a wonderful woman. But I was caught in a prison system whose nature was designed to treat adults as children.

The theory is: people who did not know how to conduct themselves and abide by the rules of society should be taken from society and reformed to act as responsible adults. If all things were fair or at least even, this would be a noble idea. All things are not fair or even. The line of victims and victimizer is often blurry. So when you oppress then condescend and patronize grown men and women, hostility and anger are usually the outcomes. Or you develop adults who act like the children the system demands.

Tragedy either makes us grow or destroys us. With God's grace, the death of my son, my worst tragedy, helped me to begin to see my life and live my life as God's gift. So much of what I was seeing around me was a curse that was affecting myself, my family, my community, my city, my state, my country, my world. I had to change. I had to do my part. The need was urgent and the task was daunting. Yet beyond the enormity of the task, doing nothing was no longer an option. The loss of my son dictated that I improve our world. I must continually find and use that strength. The love I have been so blessed to receive demands I do all I can at each opportunity.

Our greatest lessons come through our greatest tragedy.

FIT TO KILL: A REACTIONARY EXISTENCE (PART TWO) / Malakki

I was sent to death row in SCI-Greene. I battled my inner demons and fought through my mental anguish by trying to focus on being at peace with myself and consoling the few family members who were still actively supporting me with their prayers and occasional letters. My mother continued to be my rock.

One day I caught myself standing at the door of my mind while standing at the cell door. It was the summer of 1996, and I had been on death row a little over a month. I stood at the door because the cell was as empty as my plan of action in regards to what exactly I was going to do while I waited for the state to kill me.

As I stood there, I concluded that I could either get better or get worse, and either way, I would never leave prison again. This led me to the realization that my decision would truly be formed in a complete vacuum: whatever I decided, it would only affect me, but would dictate how I wanted to be on the earth my last days alive.

I had gotten myself to the worst place in a prison—the worst place on Earth for both me and my family. And it wasn't just the senseless brutality of killing a man and severely injuring another one that got me there. This act was predicated by a dim worldview that made it way too easy to point a firearm at a person and pull the trigger. And bad company, which is known to spoil good habits, had helped me steer the course to a perfect Hell.

As I sat in solitary confinement, drowning in my thoughts day after day, it dawned on me that there was something else that had helped to land me into the dark oblivion of the row. And as I searched for a way to describe and better understand this "something else," it seemed to me that this was the driving force behind my actions more than anything else.

One day I was taken out of the cell, hands cuffed and legs shackled, to a small room to be checked by a physician. It was a trial getting up on the doctor's exam table while in cuffs and shackles, but once I got situated he pulled out this tiny mallet and struck me on my knee. I said, "Why did you . . ." and my words stopped as I watched my lower leg rise and fall. I remembered getting the same type of tap on the knee from the military doctors almost a decade earlier when I was in the Army, but this time I realized something new. "Do it again," I said to the physician, and after he looked at one of the guards and received a nod he struck me again. And again my lower leg rose and fell. After the exam, I contemplated what I had seen in the reaction of my leg when my knee was hit, and why it affected me the way that it did.

Shortly after this, they moved me to a new cell. Although death row was solitary confinement and usually as quiet as a cemetery, sometimes inmates talked to each other through the air vents.

I overheard a conversation that an old head named Papa, who was in one of the cells next to me, was having with someone in an upstairs cell (only four cells shared a vent). That's when I found out that Papa had been in the Black Panther Party for Self-Defense back in the day.

When we got our hour outside in the cages, they put him in a cage beside me. I struck up a conversation with him, and he was very cordial. Somewhere in the midst of our conversation I said something like what me and my peers were doing in the streets was the same thing the Panthers were doing: we had guns, wore camo and leather jackets, and some of us even sported afros. Like I said, he was very cordial, so he didn't just tell me to shut my young, dumb-ass mouth.

First, he talked about some of the similarities, and then he spoke at length about the differences. Key among the things that separated us from the Panthers was that they came together to help and defend their communities, not destroy them. When we got back inside, I sat by the vent and listened as he went into the Black Panthers *raison d'etre* or cause for existence—for the people—and he compared it with the street *raison d'etre*—for self. He ended the discussion saying something like, because the Panthers' actions were supposed to be about a higher principle, their actions were revolutionary. And because we were just reacting to our environments, that's what made us "reactionary."

I looked at my knee, and I said that I think I understood what he meant.

What I did to get to death row was not only illegal, it was wrong. You might even say that it was evil. But it was not an action. And when I was in court, whenever the assistant district attorney or the judge started with, "Mr. Bolden's actions . . ." I knew my face showed displeasure.

This wasn't primarily because of what they were saying; it was in how they were saying it. And at the time, I couldn't understand my displeasure, let alone communicate it to someone. Simply put, it wasn't an action that brought me to death row; it was a reaction. My choice to commit crime was sort of like a veto on our social system. At the time, I couldn't accurately describe what I was doing, other than I knew I chose to "push back" against a system that I felt was seeking to grind me into the ground. My reaction to the environment I lived in was more like a tantrum, and there is no right way for a grown man to have a hissy fit.

When I speak of what I did as a reaction and not necessarily an action, I'm not using some fancy word play, trying to manipulate semantics, or find some slick angle to mitigate my crime. I shouldn't have killed that man or shot the other one, and I wish I could undo it. I can't. But if I can have a better understanding as to why I did what I did, then maybe I could help not only myself but someone else experiencing what I went through. Maybe.

With the occasional help of Papa, I sat in solitary trying to figure out exactly what happened to me. And there were times I got to talk to Harum and Calvin X because, even though we were on separate pods, we were still allowed to coordinate our visits to the cell they kept the law library in.

In time, I was able to make some sense out of my choices in a way that might resemble the way that the National Transportation Safety Board investigates a plane crash: putting emotions to the side in order to find out *why* this happened, so that it will *never* happen again. As I sought to follow Papa and turn my condemnation into a catalyst for inner tranquility, my remorse only grew. It never felt right for me to let go of the fact that I killed someone and severely hurt someone else.

Following Papa's example, I began educating myself even though the state planned to kill me. The crux of the idea came from what had happened to me at Camp Hill with the IQ test, but Papa gave me examples of how it could be done. I didn't want to die in the ignorant state I was in, especially when I had the potential to do better. There were times in the past when I used the excuse POME (Product of My Environment) to justify my behavior. In trying to overcome that state of mind, I realized that I have a choice, regardless of my environment. I could choose to be a Product of My Expectations.

There were other men on A-block who were on the same time as Papa, and whenever the COs put me in an outside cage near one of the positive men, I would try to learn something from them and ask them what they were reading or studying. One of the best things about their circle is that it included Black, White and Hispanic men and about every religion you could imagine.

My mother started sending me twenty dollars every month so I could buy soap, toothpaste, deodorant, etc., but I began to save some of it to purchase books from the addresses of the publishers I got from the men. I also began to write: poetry, short stories, or just my thoughts. It seemed like the more I read, the more I learned and wrote. . . . It was like, the more I did these things, the "whys" started losing their power over me.

And soon I was able to make peace with not only myself but with a way to be in the world that wasn't counterproductive to my existence. I also studied the law. Although I had remorse for my actions, I still filed an appeal because of advice I received from my lawyer.

It was not until later that I found out that people who did crimes similar to the one I committed got a lot less time in prison than I did. With the help of a pro bono lawyer (he represented me for free), I was able to get my sentence reduced from death to life after five years on death row. I was removed from solitary confinement and placed in general population.

THE VISIT / Oscar

One of the most important aspects of mental stability in prison is the visit. For one to know that someone still has love for them despite being in prison can go a long way. For me, a visit is a chance to come back to reality a little. To talk about something going on outside of here is always a good thing. I've met one of my nephews and two nieces on a visit. For a child who really doesn't know why you're here, it can be especially tough, and then when it's time to leave they want you to come with them. For me, some of the most important visits are the ones with my mother. To know someone loves me no matter what can go a long way in here, but to also know that every second of those visits is special because mom won't be around forever. For a mother to see her son locked up when she had so many hopes and dreams for him can create a sense of helplessness that can't be put into words.

Another type of visit for me is the "female friend" visit. Over the years I've had ex-girlfriends and "female friends" come to visit, and those types of visits can also be bittersweet. But just to be able to have someone to talk to on another level can go a long way for one on the inside. The hardest part of these visits is trying to abide with the rules during those visits. But I just wanted to give a glimpse of an important aspect of our lives in here and the visit plays a big role in our identity in here. I count it a blessing to get visits because we all know everyone in here doesn't get visits. For me the most important visits are with my family, because friends come and go, women move on, but my constant is my family. So the visit plays a big role in maintaining my connection to the outside world. It also lets me get some positive energy and encouragement to keep on going, knowing someone would take time out to come and see me.

THE RESOLUTION / Khalifa

Our God Jehovah…

I DO solemnly resolve before God to take full responsibility for myself, my wife and my children.

I WILL love them, protect them, serve them, and teach them the Word of God as the spiritual leader of my home.

I WILL be faithful to my wife, to love and honor her, and be willing to lay down my life for her as Jesus Christ did for me.

I WILL bless my children and teach them to love God with all of their hearts, all of their minds, and all of their strength.

I WILL train them to honor authority and live responsibly.

I WILL confront evil, pursue justice, and love mercy.

I WILL pray for others and treat them with kindness, respect, and compassion.

I WILL work diligently to provide for the needs of my family.

I WILL forgive those who have wronged me and reconcile with those I have wronged.

I WILL learn from my mistakes, repent of my sins, and walk with integrity as a man answerable to God.

I WILL seek to honor God, be faithful to His church, obey His Word, and do His will.

I WILL courageously work with the strength God provides to fulfill this resolution for the rest of my life and for His glory.

"As for me and my house, we will serve the Lord." —Joshua 24:15

LOCK UP MY BODY NOT MY MIND / Oscar

I'm captured like a specimen never pretended to be better than but I just am a Just man In an Unjust land So take a Good look this is better than what you read in a book Go ahead and give me those dirty looks because that is the fuel to my fire The fire that once sparked while I was in the dark created a beast Untamed and driving in the fast Lane and Never looking back to the past but full steam ahead to the level of a genius in intricate thought and action Never to be contained but shared with all Since the fall when they left me for dead saying its over we got your Body But We can Never get your mind.

CHAPTER 4
RESTORATION

CAN U STAND? / Oscar

CAN you stand when all else has fallen? How do you know you have fallen? Is it a physical thing or mental?

CAN you tell when all is Lost or do you pretend to keep it all together? Who determines the state of your being you or someone else? Are you a free thinker or are you programmed? Can you survive under the status quo or do you get up and go?

CAN change happen overnight?

OR do you stand by and watch others' plight? And say that's a damn shame they have to feel that pain. But not me, I'm free or Am I? You can't buy the supply you think you need to feed your Me! But the good news is it's free if you will open your eyes and see that the me cannot be achieved without a degree of dignity if you can stand.

PLAYING CARDS WITH MEN IN CAGES (IN FOUR CONNECTNET EMAILS) / Oscar

Most of the writings in this book were written by the men to be read aloud at weekly Elsinore Bennu meetings at SCI Pittsburgh. A few, including this one, were written after SCI Pittsburgh was closed, and the men sent to other prisons. The group then communicated through the prison email system, ConnectNet. People incarcerated in separate prisons in Pennsylvania are not allowed to communicate with each other, so all of these communications are to outside members of Elsinore Bennu—in this case, Elaine Frantz.

The email system limits the length of each email, and each incarcerated person is charged $.25 to send each email, so this essay cost Oscar a dollar to send (about three hours of prison wages).

Email One

So, speaking of the unit I used to work on, it was formally a death row unit, so you can imagine security-wise the unit. Everyone had their own cell and there was a room we called the group room and inside that room were eight single-man cages. I would go to each cell with a group list and whatever pod was eligible for group that day, I would go to each cell door and ask the person are they attending group and if so, I would write their name on the list and turn the list in to the COs. They would come out with cuffs and go to each cell and cuff the people and then they would be put in the single-man cages in the group. Sometimes, guys would change their minds and would allow someone else to take their spot. Once the group room was full, me and my boss, who was a civilian, would come in once the men were secured. We would either bring a TV in with movies to watch, or we would pull a table up and open the slots in the cages and play cards that way.

Other things I would do is if the men were in the yard cages, the kind you would see on like a jail show, I would come out with a portable radio and play music for the men and just go cage to cage and talk to people.

Now the dynamic is what I really want to get into, because my relationship with the inmates is what is important now that I have given you the visual of how the unit was set up. The building of relationships is the hard part; gaining trust from the men is the most important. Basically, the men have to know they can trust you, and the only time I was required to inform staff is if someone threatened self-harm or to harm someone else. So, yeah, a lot of the men were severely mentally ill, came from serious abuse backgrounds, and stuff like that. A lot of men hated the COs because some would play mind games with the men, and not all, because some were really good, but you always have a few so maybe in my next email I can share a few stories about how the men would view me.

Peace!!

Email Two

I forgot to also tell you to have a safe trip and a fun one, which I'm sure you will have out there. I hear Seattle is really a nice city! OK, so I spoke of the dynamic between me and the men on the SRTU unit where I used to work. I began to get to know some of the guys up there and they would look forward to seeing me. Someone who is in solitary confinement just likes to see something different sometimes, and me coming up there was the highlight of some of their days. The guys had trouble getting along with each other sometimes and would be arguing and yelling at each other, so conflict resolution was a big part of my job as well. When I would come up everyone wanted to talk to me all at once and just, say two guys weren't getting along and I was at the one's door, the other one would say don't talk to him he did this or that, and I would have to explain to them that I treat everyone equal. The system on that unit was designed to be a phase system. Phase Four was the highest, and through doing groups and positive adjustment you could phase out of the program completely. Now, that wasn't easy for a lot of them, due to anger issues with the COs so, say they cussed a CO out, then it would go in their file and count against them in the program. One day a guy could be Phase Two, allowed to the group room with no cuffs and working towards graduation from the program, and the next time I see them they are Phase Four and starting all over and I would ask what happened and the one guy would say the CO was talking to him crazy and he cussed him out or would refuse to turn in a tray after eating and would have to be cell-extracted. To some of the COs' credit, they worked in a very hostile and dangerous environment, but at the same time, it was a unit that was designed for treatment with psychology staff and CPS and different activities going on so a good CO could find the balance between all the points.

Email Three

Another issue for me I noticed was there was this pod on that unit that we called the "shit pod." The human body odor was to a point I'd never smelled up until that time. This was the Phase Four pod. Some of the most severe guys were on this pod, and that was the pod they would send guys to if they messed up and get set back in the program. And you have to remember, some guys never phased off Phase Four, and the more severe cases were over there. Now, some of them were non-verbal. A whole lot were very low IQ, and so low they would meet the mentally disabled standards. Most of them wouldn't shower and would have to sometimes be forced to shower or bribed to shower with coffee or candy.

So I would make my rounds over there and most wouldn't talk, but one guy who was over there I got along with, "Smitty," he was very low IQ and from Philly but would communicate and come to group sometimes. One day I was doing my rounds and he was kicking his door and I said what's wrong and he got up on his sink and said he was going to jump and the sink is only two feet off the ground you know and they would give him a cup of coffee to settle him down, but as far as I'm concerned, he shouldn't have been in prison along with a whole lot more up there.

You know I can remember one guy who was severely mentally ill who was going to max out his sentence, meaning no parole. Sentence complete. He was very sick, and was released, and about two weeks later killed someone, so . . .

The system is broken and I'm not bashing the Department of Corrections in this, but society's view and stance toward mental health has to change. The DOC was given the task of dealing with this and to put it like this, imagine taking your house and making it into a McDonald's restaurant. That is what prison in this state has had to do retrofit parts of certain prisons into mental health facilities and then at the same time maintain security and on the other hand change the mentality of people who have been doing stuff a certain way for so long.

Email Four

Back to my analogy of your house becoming a McDonald's restaurant: you would tell Charlotte and your Man and your son, "Hey we are still going to live here but this is also a McDonalds now." You see what I'm trying to say? So yeah, just me working up there for one year was my trial by fire.

There was this guy who was on what is called "restricted release," meaning he deemed a security risk and only [John Wetzel, the Pennsylvania Secretary of Corrections] himself can rule on him. This guy was on this because he was a sexually violent prison rapist and whenever released would prey on young white men and rape them, so he supposedly had AIDS and was dying of pancreatic cancer and he was placed in this area that was basically observation cells. They actually were the cells they used to use once someone's death warrant had been signed. So I came up for work one day, reported to the COs that I was on the unit, and noticed a tray in the hallway. The CO said, "Hey, so-and-so wants to talk to you—he keeps covering his camera in his cell," which you can't do, because he was under observation. I went to the cell area and pulled a chair up, and he said, "Hey O, do you know if they passed dinner out yet?" And I said I would ask. Now, a quick point is you had to keep your word up there. If I said I would check on something, I always did, and even if the answer is no I would tell the guys, "Look, I asked but it was a no." This was very important towards the dynamic I was speaking about. So I went to the CO and asked, "Hey, so-and-so told me to ask about dinner," and they said they already did it and this and that, but clearly I see the guy's tray sitting out in the hallway, so I went back to the guy and said they said they already did it this and that so . . .

You know, the guy was dying. Yes, he was a vicious person, but was on very powerful drugs which required him to eat, and it wasn't my place to get involved. I can't give him a tray, you know? But that was another dynamic. I couldn't get involved in situations like that because of my status, but would always keep my word, and that day I don't know if the guy ate but I can draw my own conclusions to that.

Like I said, some of the guys were more problematic than others. I remember one time I opened the door to the group room and two female psychs were in there and doing a group, and one guy in the cages was making inappropriate comments, and I spoke up and said it was inappropriate and the guy got mad and later, once group was over and I was standing in the hallway, the guy was being taken back to his cell in restraints and lunged at me. The C.O. grabbed him, but the guy apologized later on, which was nice.

Some pretty serious self-harm incidents I witnessed and that will always stick with me, you know. I don't want to gross you out on those! So yeah it was an experience and not easy. But to staff's credit, they were grateful for the work I did up there. Sometimes, they would be ready to perform a cell extraction—you know, that is where they get in riot gear and forcefully remove someone from their cell, and sometimes they would call for me and I would go up and be able to reason with the person sometimes.

One particularly bad self-harm person, he had so much scar tissue built up on his stomach that he could take a rusty paint chip of the windowsill and cut himself. It got so bad he ended up getting a septic infection and got real sick. Sometimes if he didn't get his way or whatever, he would want attention and this and that. Some guys did it from just being stressed out, but after working up there, some guys were more comfortable being in solitary confinement and have become so anti-social that they couldn't function or didn't want to be in the general population.

HELPING INMATES / Shawn

I really wanted to get involved with helping inmates who were doing short sentences because I first came to prison when I was nineteen with a six- to fourteen-year sentence. When I was in prison that first time, there were no older inmates teaching me about getting my life together. So I played sports and hung out in the prison yard with other young "boys," learning nothing about becoming a man. Then I had my sentence reduced to three to seven years because it was my first time in prison. I was not prepared to be released back into society. The prison didn't help me, and I didn't help myself. So I actually came home from prison worse then I went in. After being home for almost three years on parole, I was sent back to prison with this life sentence.

Back in prison, I would see young black man after young black man coming to prison. Because of a friend I met at SCI-Pittsburgh, I came to realize that I could possibly help these young men who were getting out on parole change their lives and give them the advice on how to stay out of prison. So with the help of the prison institution and my friend, we started a program for young men to talk about issues that could help them change the way that they look at things in their lives. We talked about being young fathers. We talked about responsibility and just being a "good person" overall. Then I was asked by staff at the institution to be a part of the Inside/Out program. After being a part of these programs, I knew this was something I wanted to do and needed to do. Whether I am released from prison, I want to make a difference in someone's life. If I can save one young man from coming back to prison once they are released, then I feel I am making a difference. Also, I want my daughter to remember me as a man who helped people instead of the person that brought me to prison. I come to understand that most young black men who come to prison did not have a father figure in their life. So they need a good black man to look up too. Hopefully I'm him.

TRYING SOMETHING DIFFERENT / Fly

When I first came to prison, I was a young man with 55 to 110 years left to do.

I didn't know nothing about the law or how it worked . . . I fell into the same stuff I was doing on the outside—getting high and making money. I became a bookie. Also, I was always looking for a way to escape, asking myself how can I do this much time?

For the first seven years, that's all I did.

Then one day I looked around and notice that the people I was hanging out with were all going home. That's when I start thinking about making some type of changes to the stuff I was doing and how I was living my life, because I wanted a chance to go home too. I stop getting high and start going to the law library, going to school and start taking groups that the prison said I had to take.

Now this change didn't come overnight. I was still booking football and basketball tickets: I wasn't ready to stop trying to make money. But I stopped running with the people that got high all the time and didn't want nothing out of life.

As I start making changes in my life, about two and a half years later, a couple of staff members started looking at me different. One day I was asked if I would help facilitate a group. At first, I said no because I didn't want to look like a sellout. I was asked to think about it. About a week later, a lady (Dr. Sand Vunojvich) who I have the utmost respect for told me that she thought that it would be a good idea for me to try something different. So that's when I started to help facilitate groups. I must say she was right because I started liking what I was doing.

As time went on, I started doing groups without the help of staff members. Over the years, I have taught Citizenship, Violence Prevention, Thinking for a Change, and Alcohol and Drugs. I took all these classes before I was able to teach them, not just so I can teach them, but to help myself in places that

I needed help.

After that I started working with the men in the Special Needs Unit. That is where they house the men who have mental health problems or who have some kind of problem that keeps them from dealing with the day-to-day functions of prison. By working with the men in that unit and seeing what kind of results that I had, I started to try and talk to some of the young men who came to prison for the first time and help them adjust, telling them about the mistakes that I made when I first came to prison, about getting high, not going to the law library to work on my case, just playing sports, not going to school, and how I wasted seven years of my life. Some of them listened, and some thought I was just a sellout working for the prison, but as long as I was helping a couple of them I was okay.

About 2013, I took a job as a Certified Peer Specialist (CPS). I had to go through training for the job, but it was something that I was already doing. A CPS is a person who can provide support to a person who is struggling with the some of the following: (1) being separated from family and loved ones, (2) an addiction, (3) depression, (4) a mental health diagnosis, (5) their sentence, (6) the crime they committed, and (7) adjusting to being incarcerated because prison life can be difficult.

A couple of the things that I let them know is that we all need to realize that there is hope and we have the ability to overcome the challenges that face us. And no matter who we are or what we did, the road to freedom starts with remembering who you are and using your strengths to become all that you are meant to be.

One of the main things that I do is use the word "we." That way, the person that I'm helping doesn't feel alone. Most of the time they just need someone to listen to them. So now I spend my days going around talking to people seeing if I can help them. You would be surprised to see how much just talking and listening to someone helps them.

THE TALKING GAME / Khalifa

I was just thinking, in light of the recent polarization surrounding the police and community—specifically the black and poorer communities—the need for conversation has again come to the forefront. Now, personally I think as many others do that this conversation is long overdue and in my mind is also bullshit because it's a conversation that's never going to result in any meaningful solutions. I am however deeply concerned as to when you're going to have the needed conversation about accountability! The one about "no one is above the law." The one that actually punishes police with equal zeal when they break the law themselves. And here is why I can't get into a conversation thing with you about it:

1) You always want to talk when you're under fire about the disclosures of profiling, racial harassment and reparations.

2) The politically-crafted laws that fostered tough-on-crime were the catalyst for mass incarceration which disassembled citizen rights, further assaulted by the Patriot Act, supported by the passing of the fake-ass drug law, then the inhuman law established to lock up juveniles without the possibility of parole. I mean it's archaic enough to even conceive a sentence of this nature, let alone impose it, and to ignore the originators of such brutal terror and corruption is mind-blowing to me. Or at least for years it was!

3) What politician in his or her right mind is going to actually address the ills of American inequality with a moral standard that is surely going to end their power-seeking bid? It really does start at the top and the subject "police killing people of color and poor" is certainly nothing new and its roots are at the core of America's freedom.

So please, somebody of moral rectitude and honesty tell me what in the hell are we supposed to talk to the death-stalkers themselves about? And why should anyone believe anything they say now? Surely the police ain't going to say, "Hey, exactly why are we pressing people of color so hard for the same crimes white people do and get away with?"

The decision-makers have a grip on the minds, laws, and principles of most Americans. They think they're free, based on the smoothness of their lives compared to others (blacks for sure) and are often reminded to be glad you're not in the shape or boat they (we blacks) are in. Some even veer off into philosophical movements, but are rarely daring enough to confront the realities of the corrupt system that holds their lives and dreams together.

And then the educated colored dude will reflect and speak, but the memories of the fates of blacks who stood all the way up press them back to the reality of the ice-cold world. They fall short of using their arsenal to uncover the morbid facts of the system they know all too well. Every black bona-fide leader has a gravesite already in this country! Every angry voice raised causes the media to erect his or her past and crush and discredit them before any significant traction is mustered. Most all of our young vanguard is in prisons or on parole. Our women are left alone to care for and protect a man-child, and the brothers who are still out there feel it is just an open opportunity to establish a harem!

So, from a group of people who first suffered from plantation psychosis, to a fearful separated individualism, to a drug-saturated numbness cursed with an identity problem, to an ignorance of our real enemy, just what on earth are they expected to say and who is going to listen!

It is not my intent to express loss of hope or to ostracize anyone. I wish someone with both heart and intact manhood would just say, "This is the black community's agenda. If you ain't with this then you're against us!" And begin to build your (our) people's future without so much dependence on the gifts and trade-offs of your people's lives. As they say in the streets, "Man-Up or Shut-up!"

NO ROOM FOR GAMES: A LETTER TO JAMILLA WITH AN ENCLOSED ESSAY / Khalifa

The names in this letter have been changed for privacy.

Hi Baby,

I seriously pray you are at peace. I am also hoping you don't allow our daughters' situation referring to Chris' playing games—to creep into anything between us! I am not Chris and I am not a child! I Love You! Just You! Ain't no room for games!!!! Especially where our hearts are involved. Listen, I believe you love me. I believe I am as important to you as you say I am. What I fear you don't understand is that you are equally (no, more than) that to me!

So let me reiterate something to you: I am totally dependent on you on your word, on your loving me, on the plans and hope we have mutually expressed concerning our future together, and by no means am I going to let *any of yesterday's bull interfere with the most sincerest and honest love I've ever had!* Please stop the fear mongering. I am ALL YOURS! And I ain't going nowhere without you beside me. We are in this together, for Life dear!

Please, you do have all the love I got. Receive it, I don't want nobody but you.

[Enclosed Essay]

How in the world can we forget when the ocean of tears still chill the bones of the lives lost and sacrificed. How innocent babies were denied life and mothers raped of both pride and identities. How can we be expected to overlook the centuries-ago terror imposed upon us, all for the economic growth of a country that now claims it wasn't their fault! Why are we called upon to forgive so damn much pain caused by an insidious group of murderers who now wish to sit in boardrooms and discuss moving on. I mean, do I look that damn forgetful? Do you really think I've lost my mind for real? Did someone tell you I never heard of those acts inflicted upon my great-great-grandfathers and mother's mothers? And didn't you know that someday the truths of your plantation exploits would reach my ears and in spite of your attempts to whitewash them with tales of respectful honor and dignity, coated with perseverance that I should focus on rather than the atrocities and move on with pride! Am I not to remember the underground railroad that again mandated the giving of lives for the simple possession of a right to life you enjoyed—but quite frankly never deserved! At least from a moral standpoint!

And what about the thousands of lives, dreams, accomplishments and contributions you buried in the mines you kidnapped us and forced us to work in till death claimed our bodies? Didn't you think one day I was going to figure out your Declaration of Independence had nothing to do with the dawning of your moral awakening? Instead, it was driven by your building fear of numbers of peoples you've mistreated for so very long, and without humane justification. And you still refuse to believe I know about the origin of your Jim Crow laws, made to justify your intentional enslavement and denial of rights so called given in your equal rights law!

The tears run deep, my friend, from the bombings in Birmingham to the lynchings in Alabama! From the shooting of Fred Hampton to the assassinations of El Hajj Malik Shabazz and Martin Luther King. Oh, I have wanted to forgive you, I have wanted to move on—but you just keep on giving with the same old shit thinking I can't smell you yet! Well, I do and you want to know something: I know you still operate on the same mindset you did in Pretoria, South Africa, when you invaded and killed all the men! Leaving behind woman and children! I know you do because you still commemorate and raise German Shepherd dogs and claim them to be trained instruments of your law, reducing the danger(s) to police officers! Bullshit! They like their masters are trained assassins, specifically used in finding and biting the enemy! Of whom you have always defined me (people of color) to be. And even in my pursuit of a means to forgive you, my looking to Jesus in the context you presented him in, I found how you twisted his words to again further satisfy your greed and fear and plain blood-thirsty yearnings towards those who did not look like you or comply with your direction.

In every walk of human advancement, I see you looming up front, on the sidelines, in the rear, watching for those who disagree with your direction, and you are just as quick to murder them as you were since the beginning. Instead of using slavery, or Jim Crow violation, or trespassing, or threat to government safety, or lack of patriotism, or war on drugs, or gang affiliation, or plain "stand your ground" shit, you kill us! For something you perceived! Not a reality: your fear(s). Your lynchings now come under the guise of "You felt threatened." Well, I got news for you dude: You've threatened me all my f---in' life for no reason except some shadows of your evil you can't get past, but I'm not scared of you no more! Your disregard of my birthright are reflected in Philadelphia, where you dropped a bomb on innocent women and children. None of y'all went to jail! In Rosewood, under the guise of a white women being raped, despite the numerous black women you've filled history pages of with the same act! Nobody went to jail! Oklahoma bombing of Black Wall Street, just because my people were succeeding without your involvement, again no one arrested for the infamous Tuskegee experiments, settlements used to hush the suits filled long after most victims were dead!

So just what do you want to talk about now? You want to tell me that you are going to improve upon police training. Well, you can tell your cadets all sorts of law-binding rules; they didn't listen to you then and they won't listen to you now. See, I know this is again some media. By some time, they'll forget and forgive, they'll come around at the mention of some money and another social program accompanied with a promise. But there's no accountability from the voices spouting that rhetoric! Because they listen to the rulers—the powerful. Besides, this has been a thought out plan since the days of Willie Lynch! Only the modern tactics of application have been revived; the intent, the control, the racism, the fear, and the primitive beast mentality that gave birth to this genocide of people of color remains a means of sport and show of superiority for a white system of God-players.

I'm certain you don't want to talk about injustices nor about the war on drugs (otherwise known as "legalized hunting and enslaving people of color and poor") for sure you don't want to discuss mass incarceration, not after you've touted the need for public safety to disguise your assaults and killings of unarmed black youth! I'm convinced of your sickness when you decided it was more important to close schools and build more prisons and lo and behold you had to rewrite laws to increase criminal law codes to fill them and this was top legislative priority cause votes and cabinet seats are more important than people's lives and families, and especially black communities and education.

Two things I'm certain you don't want to talk about is reparations and prosecution of legislators who have knowingly and for personal financial gain conspired to undermine the United States Constitution and civil rights laws! Naw, you don't want to bring up the good ole-boy Supreme Court justices nor the criminal court judges or the federal court judges who know your laws and refuse to raise legal objections to the height of law suits to thwart the progressive machine of colonial slavery sanctioned by law. How in the world am I to believe anything you guys say!

[Jamilla,]

This is where my thoughts be when not on you. I don't have time to waste while these folks are killing our children's dreams, nor do I believe for one minute that they are not thinking of some other plan of mass destruction to impose upon the errant young black youth or those who believe in the American dream!

No, I can't change the world, but I can write and tell anyone reading about what I think about the world we live in and hope some of our young men and women will read and begin to actually see what's going on around them and quit trusting these damn white folks so much! They are intentionally dumbing down our children and it is our responsibility—a man's obligation to forewarn our youth. After which they can decide for themselves! But our youth deserve to know the truth!

So, that's where I am when apart from you. I'm angry. I'm honest and I guess I'm a bit crazy to think I can make a difference!

One thing I know for sure, a good man needs a good strong woman with him, and that woman for me is YOU!!!!!!!!!!! So just let me love you please, for the first time in my life. I have all I need, My Jamilla...

I Love All of You Sugar,
And That's Real!!!!

CONSIDER THE FIST / Malakki

When conflict comes and your physical space is tested,
you consider the fist even without it being suggested.
In the fight for your manhood with all its turns and twists,
this struggle is mostly mental, but you should still consider the fist.

First consider the thumb; up or down, life or death,
now consider the margin between first and last breaths.
Pointed to the side, the thumb resembles the dash,
between the birth date and death date on a tombstone's slab.
The whole story of your life in that little-bitty line,
after your death, there's only one way that this can be defined.
Once you're in the ground, the only you that can occur,
is from the experiences of those who met you; only this speaks to
what you were.
When you pull that thumb in to clench the four fingers it makes strong,
it's like a good reputation remaining to others once you are gone.
So when you disrespect others and live life in pride's midst,
I want to remind you to please, please consider the fist.

Consider the pointer, for its use it seems bigger,
used to tickle your child, but also used to pull the trigger.
For a proud father whose child's laughter is like a drug, is one use,
the other is a community-killing lost-soul defending a rep,
pushing drug abuse.
You may see no contradiction in using the pointer finger for both
these things,
until you're in court and somebody points the finger at you and
starts to sing.
Then here comes the explanation that actually fails to truly
explain,
why your child is without a father filled with so much pain.

When you close your hand and the pointer and thumb kiss,
this brings a unification of purpose so please, consider the fist.

Consider the middle finger and what the "F" it stands for,
raising it to the sky is the perfect recipe for war.
It stands rugged alone, although it can be easily broken,
but when joined with the pointer, peace is always spoken.
A stronger message together and one way to let this linger,
think of the "peace sign" as you giving the middle finger to the
trigger finger.
A man who lives a life of peace will be rated high on anyone's list,
one who lives the middle finger fails to truly understand the fist.

Consider the ring finger and all that is meant,
to give your word to a woman and to her you live to represent.
The ring finger is special and what sets it apart,
is that it holds a vein that is connected straight to the heart.
So when you violate your trust and break the bond of the wedding band,
this reaches your heart, now the deception is in your hands.
This finger starts a family, don't disrespect this,
because without this finger, you can't even consider a fist.

Now, consider the pinky finger and because of its size,
it may be looked down on, disrespected or despised.
The first to be overlooked are those small in stature, reputation
or size,
barely making it with little money, limited skills, or who are not
too wise.
Everyone has something small about them: because of this I want
you to consider,
that making fun of someone else's shortcomings doesn't make
you bigger.
Your imperfections make you exceptional, so please consider this,

you are perfect—perfectly you—symbolically found in your unique fist.

What you do with the gift of your fists is your choice, but whatever your plan,
your actions with them will define you, this you must understand.
Consider the open palm; the perfect fit for your child's mother's hand,
as she struggles to give birth to a child that makes you feel more like a man.
The same hand used to hold your newborn daughter or son,
using the power of touch—your child's first language—a lifelong connection has begun.
But when disputes come, that same hand grabs the keys to the car,
so you can go and smack a drunk woman's ass and raise another glass at the bar.
Whether you are known as a drunk, a cheater, or an honest family man,
you will be judged by what people see you do with your hands.
Your hands will tell the story of you even when you no longer exist,
and because it's the same size as your heart; please, please consider the fist.

TALKING ABOUT RACE / Fly

How can we have a talk about police/community relations without talking about race? None of what I write can be understood until you recognize that we (African Americans) are not relevant, and we are thought of as hostile, ignorant, and a permanent threat. Until we force a change in the perception which goes way beyond improving police/community relations and really involves a national discussion on race and class, the modern-day lynchings that we see will continue.

The US is such a residentially segregated society that it is actually possible for many white people to never have to deal with black people. They may only see black people on film or television. If they are addicted to Fox News, then their perception of black males are the worst.

Perhaps we can look at the role race plays on the black child. To go through life every day having to think about how to behave so as not to scare white people, and how to walk and how to talk and how to respond to a cop (not because you're wanting to be polite, but because you like to see your mother again) is work. So race is our biggest problem.

For example, you send a white police officer, not from the community, who sees all blacks as criminals, into an all-black neighborhood. The officer may decide to start a confrontation in which a black child can end up dead or even if the child starts the confrontation, the person who ends up dead is the black person and it is called justice.

We need to get rid of the community leaders (really, community limelighters) who only come out when somebody has been killed or something bad happens. We need community leaders who are proactive, not reactive. So in dealing with police/community relationships we must start with race.

HOW POLICING CAN BE BETTER IN THE BLACK COMMUNITY / Shawn

I believe that the black communities need to be more involved with interaction with their local police department. I remember when I was about ten years old I would see signs in the windows of my neighbors' homes saying "Neighborhood Watch." Black communities need something like that to return and then take it to the next step by having neighborhood watch patrols. This will have a presence in the community, and more crimes will be witnessed as they are being committed. Another thing is that black communities need to give up the "code of silence," or of being too afraid to report a crime or be willing to testify in court. Crimes happen in front of a crowd of people and no one seems to see anything or does not want to come forward. The police don't see why they should help the community when the community will not help themselves.

I also believe that the police need to be more a part of the community, outside of just when they are working. Get to know the people of the community on a personal level, like showing up at the basketball and football games. I also believe that the police force in the black community needs to have more black officers to reflect the people of that community, because who knows their own race of people better than themselves. Black communities need to stop looking at the police as the enemy and talk to them when they see them in the neighborhood.

HUMAN RELATIONS (A SERMON ABOUT CITIES) / Khalifa

"Then the Lord came down to see the city and the tower which those men had built, and he said, Now then, these are all one people and they speak one language; this is just the beginning of what they are going to do. Soon they will be able to do anything they want! Let us go down and mix up their language so that they will not understand each other."
—Genesis 11:5-7

"When the day of Pentecost came, all the believers were gathered together in one place. Suddenly there was a noise from the sky which sounded like a strong wind blowing, and it filled the whole house where they were sitting. Then they saw what looked like tongues of fire which spread out and touched each person there. They were all filled with the Holy Spirit and began to talk in other languages, as the spirit enabled them to speak."
—Acts 2:1-4

Admittedly, there are several instances in scripture that seem to portray the city in bad light. Yet closer examination reveals that there are two distinct images of the city in scripture: one good and one bad.

The negative: the first builder of a city mentioned in scripture is Cain, the murderer who killed his brother (Genesis 4:17). There is also the story about the construction of the Tower of Babel (Genesis 11:1-9), which identifies human ambition and arrogance as key factors in the construction of the city, incurring divine wrath and spawning confusion and misunderstanding. Mentioned 260 times in scripture as a city or an empire, Babylon is the second most-frequently-referenced urban setting, and its image in this context is virtually synonymous with wickedness. From the prophet Habakkuk's complaints to the unflattering descriptions in Revelations 17 and 18, it is clear that Babylon connotes rebellion against God! This is the city as a pitfall in society.

Might Pittsburgh, Philly, Erie, Harrisburg or New York be like these cities? Bad cities in which moral dysfunction, injustice, violence, and oppression reign?

In contrast, more than one thousand references to the city of Jerusalem are made, and it is frequently portrayed as "the holy city", where God resides (Psalm 46:4, Zechariah 8:3 and Matthew 4:5). Illustrations of Jerusalem found in Isaiah 65:17-25 and in Revelations 21:1-4 reveal idealistic images in which God's presence in the city renders it safe, a healthful, and happy environment. The record of Pentecost even, which occurs in Jerusalem (Acts 2:1-12), stands in marked contrast to the Tower of Babel event. In this case, the quest to seek God's guidance replaces human arrogance and results in divine blessing and understanding.

The image of Jerusalem in scripture thus comes to symbolize what can happen when God's presence among people is rightly acknowledged and affirmed. In this city, God's glory manifests itself in the abundant evidence of social, spiritual, and material well-being found among the city's inhabitants who enjoy the abundance of God's omniscient and omnipresent love, mercy and protection. This reflection represents the presence of God in right relationships among all residents, and love, justice, and righteousness, peace and praise of God are the fruit of this city's divine character.

Those whose lives are governed by faith in God will live in such a way as to inspire right relationships in which love, justice, forgiveness, and praise of God are evident, and as such will qualitatively elevate the entire environment and atmosphere (Isaiah 4:2-6; Micah 4:1-4).

Where there is no faith in God or where such faith is tentative or of secondary importance, human relationships suffer as do environmental conditions in the city (Genesis 4: 8-12 and Luke 19: 41-44).

Brothers, the spirit asks you this morning to examine your faith! Respond to your obligations. Speak life and light into darkness, and do your part to stop the killing of our sons and daughters.

May the reading of the word be a blessing upon your heart.

THE JOURNEY TO OURSELVES / Malakki

Most on earth feel they were created from some unseen greatness mostly referred to as "God." They may define it as something far greater and more vast than anything humans can imagine. But what if this was quite the opposite? What if we didn't come from something greater that made us on a smaller scale, but we come from something smaller that extended itself into what eventually made us? In other words, people may search the sky for the holy or angelic, but the messengers that awoke life in us should be looked for in microscopes, not telescopes.

We know that Life existed as a cosmic stasis, but I posit that something within Her pushed out—as if just existing to exist wasn't enough. The way I see it, that rebellious part of Life kept pushing out until it found a way to birth itself into a new identity. It was then that Life first realized Herself in creation's mirror. She brought Herself from a non-physical essence into a physical existence.

Her offspring came into being at the micro level, which we recognize as a chemical signature. In this way, Life found a way to thrust Herself into physical order. In disorder, She kept Her stasis but remained unrealized to anything else but Herself. And what existed had no measurement or movement; not only were these things not realized, they were not necessary.

Within order, Life lost Her stasis but gained a physicality and a movement unmatched in Her prior inert perfection. At this point, She was ready.

Many who study scientific theories of creation may consider my concept uniquely explained, but in essence it is nothing new. What plunges this consideration over the precipice of the norm is the unification of scientific theory with some aspects of religious thought in my understanding that there was an inherent goal to this early form of what eventually became us . . . there was an agenda.

Unseen microorganisms communicate in ways that we do not yet understand. But we know that they transmit as well as receive specific data inherent to their functions. Knowing an astute communication exists but continues to be an indecipherable foreign language to us, and since we know it is used to bring forth such phenomenal complexities that range from childbirth to passing on the common cold, could not the objective of conspiring to build us be possible?

To me, this explains how She hears our prayers. She is not something remote or absolute from us. She is inherent in what we are.

In order to further explain my premise, I'll lend an analogy: if we were a small building in a small town, our creator wouldn't be a skyscraper in some far-away, large, metropolitan city that we should aspire to be. She would be the bricks and mortar that holds us together.

I believe that the Ancient Egyptians had an understanding of what I am proposing, and the evidence can be revealed in some of their earliest myths. In their cosmology, deity was not something separate from us and could be realized in a powerful entity like the sun, the subtle way crops burst through the earth to administer the fitness of their purpose, or something as simple as the human breath.

To reach the Ancient Egyptian's ideal human objective was a process that eventually ended in a form of apotheosis. It began when someone lived a life of balance ("Maat")—which was mostly about adhering to pro-social mores—and then lived a daily life seeking to realize their connections to all forms of Life: whether they be seen or unseen. When a person met the challenges of their life in a responsible manner, after death their soul (called "Ba") would return to the high station referred to as the "Blessed Abode."

This is a cursory view of the Ancient Egyptian's expansive pantheon, and one may find that even a basic comprehension of their philosophy seems impossible or futile. But each God and Goddess is nothing more than an attribute of Life Herself, further appreciated singularly but not truncated or removed from the conceptualized whole.

We owe the Greeks, especially Plato, for the first de-evolution of mankind's thought from an understanding of being part of a greater whole to a so-called "rationalized" concept of humans as independent, objective beings. I disagree with the idea that mankind can be considered as "thinking" beings only if they hold as sacred what can be known. And further, I believe that this puts humanity into a quandary if we only seek to objectify that which is witnessed by the five senses and realize only what is known, instead of placing adequate attention towards knowing that which has not yet been realized.

Even if some humans psychologically jump the universalized hurdle of considering themselves separate and objective from creation, they may still be bound to an understanding that the greatest height of what humans can conceive lies outside of our being.

This point of view is totally removed from the consideration that we are the sum of our creator. And that the spark of Her creative energy rekindles the connection between us in every breath we take.

When a human perceives themselves as an entity separate and unique from a greater cosmos, and further sees the natural world as an aggressive "other" that must be harnessed, controlled, or subjugated, the most one can do is possibly "conceive" of a deity instead of being at an understanding that we are at one with Her. And, in my opinion, one who follows this course will never truly appreciate Life's gift.

For a look at the deeper implications of what I am

presenting, understand that Life's connections are not only visceral but also omnipresent. And She doesn't judge us and seems to accept the best of us no matter what form of dogma we adhere to, or the lack thereof. She's just that nice. And this is despite the fact that our most popular religions would probably demonize a return to the recognition of the Almighty Her; which was referred to by the ancients as The Goddess. This may be especially so when the core principles of this concept would not be a search for what would gain us entry into another realm or dimension called heaven. Instead, the focus would be on what actions would lead us to an integrated journey to the agenda within; as well as sowing the best seeds to foster a realization of our connection to the whole of reality.

Maybe one day humans will stop dismissing our true creator and move towards a more efficacious way of being on the planet . . . we'll see.

A LETTER TO MY SISTERS / Khalifa

I apologize for all the turbulence I have caused in your life . . .
For the pain of cowardliness, when your crown(s) were denied,
for cringing in the heat of defending your dignity, turning away
from your attacker and blaming you for the assault.

Yes, I heard your cry. I saw the defiance in your eyes. I
heard resoundingly the calling of my name—felt the pounding
in your heart. How could I not. We were one, united, rising
from the same spirit. Until, that day, like sweat running down
my back, I felt my strength ebbing, I felt my stomach churn,
twisting from some vile ingestion of fear, blocking out or
smothering the voice(s)—urging me into action.

Frozen, I heard the tears fall inside my chest, putting out
the natural flame that burned of Life.

I was numb for years, decades—chasing shadows and
running from ghosts. Intoxicating my senses, denying the
reality of the genocide I watched in silence. I saw my roots dug-
up and cut-up and I saw them traded for pennies and purchased
for pleasure and worked to death and blamed for everything
that had soul.

I knew you would never surrender despite the lighter
babies, never mind the washing of everyone's clothes and your
denial of the right to vote being taken as some silent sign of
approval of the degraded life thrust upon you, spilled in you
against your will. Because I thought I'd be better off alone,
without the constant reflection in your eyes of who I am
supposed to be.

I ran and ran from plantation to castration devoid of my
mind hiding from my spirit, afraid of you, scared to think—to
know—to obey my knowledge—without asking permission!
On my own I had not the courage.

To come back to you, to rescue you, rescue me, rescue

the world, from the cancerous disease that just keeps on taking lives and killing futures and hopes and dreams, spirits!!

Finally, running out of corners where my drug mental president had me pledging allegiance to his will, at last breaking the bottom of my wine. Time to be someone else left me putting out the cigarette of no name. Just like me. I have found the path. I have heard the voices. I recognize the image looming before me, a bright ray of light piercing the darkness causing those dark loving demons to flee.

And a surging stream of heat coursing through my veins, sifting out the staleness that was suffocating me. And I feel alive, life, and strong, and eager now, like a drum. A powerful instrument to set a pace or pick up the beat . . . thumping in my heart, I'm coming, I'm coming, back to you. Coming back for you, coming to rescue you, and I no longer fear the heat of the dragons' breath, nor cringe at the flap of his wings. I no longer freeze in darkness, cause I AM the light. From darkness, all that I am supposed to be was created and burst through darkness, and I Was Named Good . . .

Forgive me sister for shunning the rock of my everlasting. Forgive me sunshine, for seeking shade after wallowing in your valley. Forgive me daybreak for dislodging my brain and allowing some sick psychological despot to create my story and bind you in fear of me.

I am Earth's goodness, dawning.

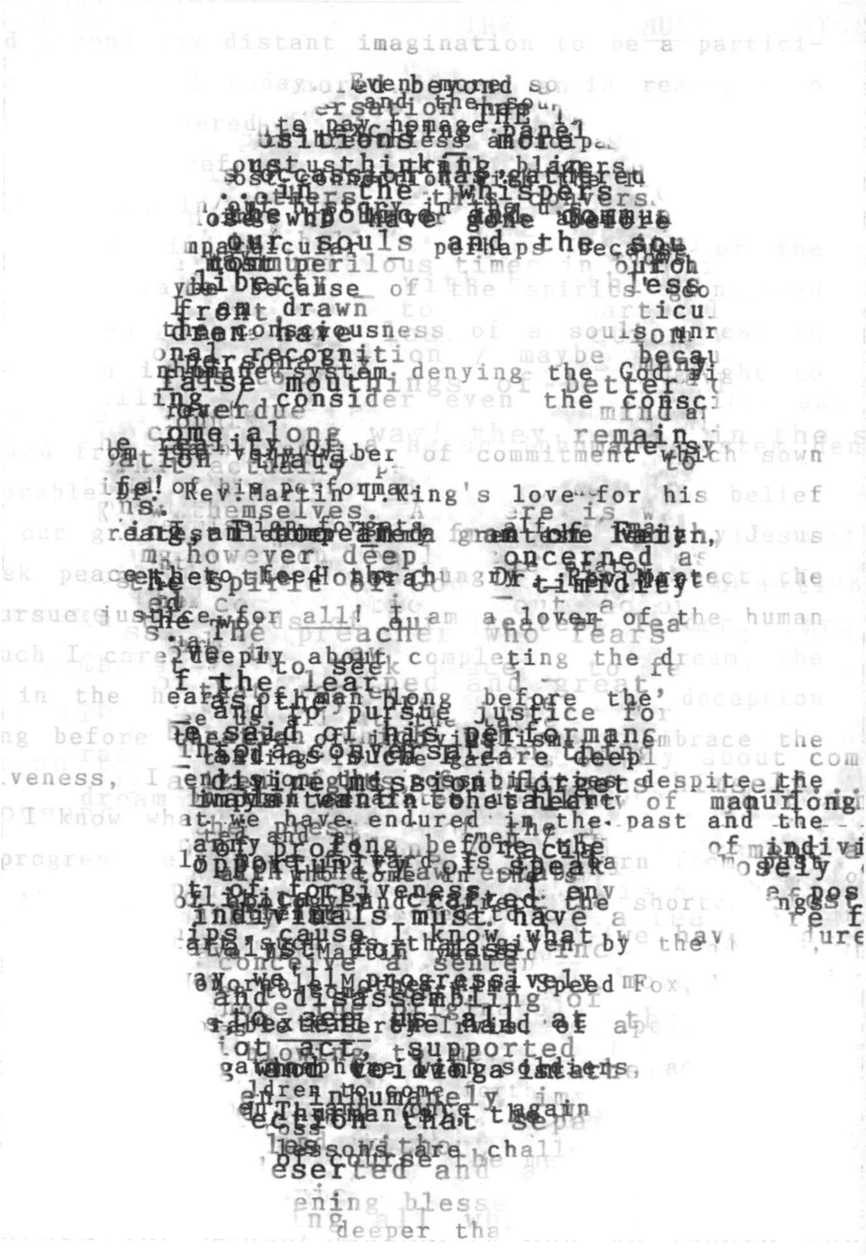

AFTERWORD: LAST DAY / John Edgar Wideman

Sometimes going to see my brother in prison is like when you hear a person call you *nigger*, a somebody you maybe don't know, a stranger who suddenly becomes intimately close by establishing a boundary line, by drawing it and crossing it simultaneously with the n-word as if the two of you, separated by his line, have known each other a lifetime, and *nigger* declaimed by him or her restores with absolute authority a prolonged, familiar, shared history whether or not you have ever laid eyes on one another before, that person with *nigger* in their mouth, drawing a line that divides, claiming a compelling relationship of intense distance, intense intimacy as if neither you nor she nor he have any means, any right or reason to deny that word *nigger* once it's up in your faces, you with no more power to erase or nullify the line or the *nigger* word than colored boys in Cleveland or New Orleans or Seattle have power to erase or nullify bullets police officers shoot into their bodies, guns fired for many of the same reasons in every case, though the news media say, and we the people say, don't we, each case is also, yes, yes, a separate case with differing, yes, extenuating circumstances, differences sometimes as obvious as difference between night and day, black and white, or different like different sounds of *nigger* depending on whose lips speak the word, differences private, public, acceptable or not in terms of law or public opinion, differing acts, but all validated by the same rule, a rule old at least as this country, a rule continuing to persist, and though we may disagree about its appropriateness or application in each circumstance, it persists predictably, along with its often unarguably fatal, direct consequences, that rule which originated when some of us in a position of power abused that advantage and enslaved people, used power's brute force to seize and imprison the bodies of others and treat them as inferiors, as if those enslaved others born members of a different group, a kind or variety or race not exactly deserving to be considered human beings, and once designated as such, treated as such, remain different forever, a rule that still rules today, dividing us into separate races, declaring that each person's designated race stays the same always, stays in force today, and though the rule may operate covertly or blatantly, it remains present every time in every case to reinforce and justify whatever other motives a person might conjure up for calling a person *nigger* or imprisoning niggers or segregating niggers or shooting many many bullets into a young nigger body, then it's too late, always too late, too long, bang, bang, victim dead, don't fuss, don't protest, the rule's the rule, a prerogative in place too long, suspects presumed guilty, no defense against being called nigger, nor do unarmed colored boys girls women men possess any magic to stop bullets that armed citizens of various colors designated as officers, deputies, cops, agents fire into them, no power except perhaps to remember always the time-honored, hoary prerogative, remember the rule of a line dividing separate races and embrace it, seize it and turn it around as self-defense, as battle-cry, use the rule to stigmatize and abuse others before they use it to hurt and destroy you, before they call you out your name.

It's never absent, though I seldom hear anyone say *nigger* out loud in the prison visiting room, the word rings in my ears each time I visit. Need it, I admit, so say it to myself in order to deal with an otherwise intolerable situation. Need it to answer a question tearing me up inside when I look around and see a busy, crowded visiting room filled mainly with people my color, the many colors of my family. Why such an overload of us in this terrible place? Why us a question with an answer I have been taught already, learned in childhood, an ancient answer known before my very first visit to a prison and known for all the visits, all the years and years since: this is the way things are, have always been, and shall be forever.

But that answer instilled when I was a boy beginning to ask questions about a world perplexing him, that answer too ordinary, not stunning enough, not satisfying enough in the prison visiting room and it gives me no peace when I try to make sense, try to account for faces surrounding me, far, far too many faces colored like mine, and no answer truly explains our disproportionate presence, nor my outrage and sense of defeat, no answer sufficient to compel me to accept the evidence my eyes confront, no answer, only confirmation of a line drawn long, long ago, before I was born, a rule that divides faces I see into two groups, unalterably divides them into two separate groups and then I am able to remind myself, say to myself, *nigger*, niggers of course, that's why, and no other explanation required, what else would I, should I, would anybody expect. *Nigger*, the word we need to shout out loud or whisper inside ourselves and that word reveals why.

The line there. Hard, rigid, premeditated as the prison visiting room's bolted-to-the-floor, plastic seats arranged side by side, in aisles and sections, all seats in each section facing in the same direction so eye contact impossible with a person beside you unless you twist in your seat, lean over a metal rail that divides one seat from the next. You talk sideways, as close as you can get to a visitor's ear. Awkward conversations, minimal privacy in an overcrowded space that also isolates. None of the humming discontent, the simmering helplessness and frustration a person experiences upon entering the prison visiting room is accidental. Room's layout conceived, like the rule to divide races conceived, in order to execute a plan. And plan works. The architecture's visible scheme—expressed by unmovable steel, by concrete of floor and ceiling, by locked doors, windowless walls—boxes you in. Visible lines repeat the ancient, invisible injunction to consider yourself either one kind of human or another kind. Choice drastically limited. No choice except to go along with a program long in place. Once entered, no exit. No way out except to scream loud enough to bring walls tumbling down. And who's prepared to spoil a visit. Prepared to risk imprisonment. To resist guards, sirens, clubs, guns. No. When you visit you follow house rules, rules posted on the walls, rules that define and reduce your choices, eliminate all other options. Nigger rules that humble and humiliate and impound.

At one end of the visiting area, far end from where my brother and I occupy adjacent seats, a play corner reserved for small children, an area supervised by an inmate and furnished with bright plastic toys. Good job, my brother says, nodding at the corner. Only trustees get it. Playing with kids. Out the goddamn cell 4 to 5 hours at a time. Wouldn't mind doing it myself, 'cept everybody knows the guys you see over there too tight with the guards. Only way you get the best jobs in here. Wouldn't let none my kids go to those guys. Don't mind me, man. Some them guys just guys like everybody else. But ain't nothing free in here.

Hungry.

You know they starve us. Always hungry. Worse since they brung in that private company and started counting calories. As if grown men supposed to exist on what those charts say enough. Everybody walk round here all day hungry. Hungry wake you up in the middle of the damn night. Shame how they do us, bro. Getting so bad some these guys kill another guy for a bag of chips.

Remembered to bring quarters this time. What's the rule now? You allowed to push buttons or not?

No, no. They see me touch a vending machine, visits over. Ass outta here.

What you want, then. Knock yourself out. Plenty quarters today.

You know I like them wings. Package of chicken wings. A cheesesteak. If they outta cheesesteaks, a double burger. Bag of popcorn if any left. And some grape juice or some kinda juice, or pop if that's all they got. Don't matter really. Junk all they put in them machines, but you know something, it tastes kinda good, brother dear, after slop they be feeding us everyday in here. And nice to feel kinda halfway filled up half a minute. Thank you.

I wait in line behind a very young, very pregnant woman who punches in choices like she's been here before, inserting quarters one by one from the see-thru bagful she holds in her off-hand. Then wait my turn at a microwave oven on a table beside vending machines. Don't turn around to look at my brother, but I listen, and our conversation starts up in my head while I wait, while he waits, and I wonder how we always find so much to say, more to say, never finish saying it.

Tape runs, etc, etc, etc in my mind . . . I hear it word by word. Visit again, smell the warmed-up bag of popcorn from the machine, taste cold apple juice, hear my brother beside me, here, there, wherever we are.

Wonder if he ever daydreams a last day, day a guard delivers clothes for outside, a paper shopping bag for transporting property my brother accumulated inside, receipts for bag and possessions he must sign, wonder if he daydreams about that day and I want to ask him what he might feel if and when, ask him what he thinks he might be thinking when the steel door of his cell slides open, Spivak or Crawford or Jones or Valdez standing there in the passageway waiting, looking at him, less curious than I am about what's on his mind, looking through him, past him, past this task to the next, one task closer to the end of same ole same ole slog of guard duties imprisoning them with him night and day until punch-out time, one guard or two, three, maybe the whole dreary crew of them, living and dead, every single officer hired and fired by the state department of corrections since day one, every single sorry one of them in uniform again to escort him down long rows of cells, through more gates, then across the yard, vacant, quiet this early, to the final gate, rank after rank of silent guards crowded into the narrow corridor just beyond his cell's open door, guards stern-faced, grinning, scornful, accusing, no, no, no, just standing, just impatient, just wanting it over with, whatever, peering through him as if he's already gone, simply not there, or there like a shit smear in a toilet bowl their duty to maintain spotless, this day of leaving no different for them than any day they are paid to watch him, their eyes, the expressionless expressions soldered on their faces giving up nothing, as his eyes, his expression give nothing back, keeping each other at a distance way too vast to cross, distance any sane person has no reason to cross and decent folk know better than even to imagine crossing because everybody understands, don't they, what's over there across the line, nothing's there, an abyss, a bottomless pit over there in which people burn up, become nothing, vanishing fast as prisoners sentenced to life supposed to vanish from life, like him, like me, though I want to believe I might escape my cell by asking him how he thinks he would feel the last day, except the idea of a last day is nothing but twist, glimmer, less than nothing as it passes too quickly to follow and disappears into the abyss, the cauldron, and to protect himself from plunging even deeper into nothingness, would he allow himself even that idle thought of freedom, freedom, an excruciating stab of pain until it's nothing again after a thought of free flies, slinks past, nothing again, he remains behind bars, in a cell, so why bother to think differently, as if inside and outside not absolutely separated, as if there's a chance of release, of being elsewhere other than where he is, nowhere, nothing, consumed, disciplined by the business of survival while he perishes here, in this nowhere place where he is, there where it's impossible for him to take me or anyone else, except maybe in daydreams he dreams in his cell, so I teach myself to resist the temptation to ask, and pretend instead that we are both inside when I visit the prison, or pretend both of us outside, pretend that words we speak, words I write bring us closer together, and for his sake and mine (my response a bit like the guards, I'm ashamed to admit) I try not to wonder too much about his daydreams, do not ask to hear them, nor ask if he ever thinks about what he might feel or do last day.

ABOUT THE WRITERS AND EDITORS

Malakki (Ralph Bolden) was born in Pittsburgh, PA. He is an Army veteran. After his honorable discharge, he worked several jobs: during nights and days off he gained some notoriety as a DJ and spoken word artist. He performed in Pittsburgh and in several other states until he lost control of the severe anxiety he began suffering from while in the military. It was in this state that he made the tragic choices that led to his incarceration. He's currently serving his twenty-fifth year of a life sentence; his incarceration began with five years on death row before his sentence was overturned by the State Supreme Court. Malakki self-educated himself during the years spent in solitary confinement. When released from death row, he became a tutor/teacher's aide for fifteen years and helped hundreds of men receive their GEDs. He recently received training to become a certified peer support specialist and now works to support prisoners with mental health challenges. He is also a published poet and author. In the 2016 PEN Writer's Awards for prisoners, he won the Dawson Prize in Fiction & Honorable Mention in Non-Fiction.

Oscar Brown was born in 1985 in Columbus, OH, one of five siblings. His earliest childhood memory is witnessing the aftereffects of his father's attempt to kill his mother. Once his mother recovered, they moved and she eventually allowed his father back into his and his brother's life. He struggled in school and got into some fights and got lots of school suspensions. School was hard for him. His father died when he was twelve, and it really impacted him. He barely graduated high school and a series of bad decisions led to his crime. He was involved in the killing of a neighborhood man who grew up one street over from him and who had some similar struggles to him: he made the decision to get involved in a beef and unfortunately that man was killed and another man was seriously wounded. Oscar was arrested at age nineteen. In the last ten years of his prison sentence, he has tried to make a serious change in his life; it started with the Inside-Out prison exchange program. He has completed Violence Prevention and various drug groups, graduated from Stratford Career Institute as a drug and alcohol treatment specialist, and is a certified peer support specialist. He is also level one Wellness Recovery Action Plan (WRAP) certified. He has been a student in numerous Inside-Out classes and is a co-founder of the Elsinore Bennu Think Tank for Restorative Justice. He is currently enrolled in International Christian College and Seminary, working towards a degree in Christian counseling. He volunteers as a Canine Partners for Life Prison pup handler, training service dogs for disabled citizens. This is who he is. His actions in January of 2005 can never be taken back: all he can do now is continue to work on his self, help others, and give back in any way that he can and show that he is not the same person that he was when he came in over fourteen years ago.

Norman Conti is a founding member and guiding spirit of the Elsinore Bennu Think Tank at SCI Pittsburgh. With the think tank, he developed the Police Training Inside-Out program in order to bring incarcerated men together with police recruits for a four-day seminar on Criminal Justice Policy. After the prison closed and the incarcerated members were scattered throughout the state, he rebuilt the Elsinore Bennu Think Tank for Restorative Justice as a weekly conference of community activists and ex-offenders to serve as a communications hub for developing and ongoing programs, especially those designed to reduce recidivism and to address the needs of vulnerable youth. Norm is a professor of sociology at Duquesne University of the Holy Spirit. He has published ethnographies of recruitment, socialization, ethics training and masculinity in policing as well as multiple analyses of the social networks that develop within recruit cohorts. He has also co-authored an article on destigmatization and book chapters on humility among activists, social crime prevention, sustained dialogue and hate crime. Norm holds a PhD in Sociology from the University of Pittsburgh.

Khalifa (Richard Diggs) also known as "Chuckie," was born on August 20, 1950. He lived with his parents and several siblings around Pittsburgh for the first years of his life. As a child, he watched his parents violently arrested by police in their home. He was also the victim of severe poverty and abuse as a child. By around 10 years old, he began to be placed in various foster homes and juvenile detention facilities. He served in the military, where he picked up a heroin addiction. He sold drugs and guns and committed many terrible violent crimes. He received a life sentence for two murders he committed in 1976 and 1977, and spent the rest of his life incarcerated, mainly at SCI-Pittsburgh. After some years in prison, he became a Christian, a minister, an activist, and a counselor and advisor to many men incarcerated with him, and (through voluminous correspondence) to many boys in Juvenile Detention facilities. He was a man of great dignity. He loved to talk about how to fix our broken world, and never had enough time to say all of the things that he needed to say. And he always had friends, to whom he was loyal. Late in life he married his life-long friend, Helen, who he called "Jamilla". Although he was in intense pain during the last year of his life, he insisted until his final days that only he could push Malakki's wheelchair. In 2017, he died of complications from late-diagnosed cancer in a hospital room, we are told on the bathroom floor. He died alone, because those who loved him were not allowed to know where he was as he died. At his funeral, those who cared about him—Helen, his children and grandchildren, friends, non-incarcerated think tank members, men who had once been incarcerated with him and considered him a mentor, and prison employees and even a police officer who had become his friends, overflowed the church.

Amber M. Epps has been teaching at the college level for over fifteen years in traditional classroom, hybrid, and online settings. Usually teaching a variety of information technology and communications courses, she has also taught other subjects including economics, business administration, and human resource management. Amber holds a Bachelor of Business Administration with a focus on Computer Information Systems from Kent State University, a Master of Business Administration with a focus on Management Information Systems from Point Park University, a Master of Science in Information Systems & Technology (Usability Studies) from South University, a Doctor of Science in Information Systems & Communications from Robert Morris University, and a Doctor of Education in Postsecondary and Higher Education from Argosy University. Outside of academia, Amber has experience working in community development, focusing on commercial district revitalization, workforce development, and youth education and employment. Furthermore, Amber has an entrepreneurial spirit, and has started an organization called LOCAL 412, which is dedicated to promoting the fact that hip hop is an art. In 2016, with her sister and best friend, she opened Arts & Crafts, a botanica and occult shop. Amber has also been referred to as the "mom of Pittsburgh hip hop," writing, producing, and performing music both inside and outside of Pittsburgh, as well as creating opportunities for other local artists and working with them to hone and develop their craft. As a music artist, in 2013 Amber was honored as a resident artist at Most Wanted Fine Art gallery. She was also recognized for her work in education, the arts, and the community by being named one of the *Pittsburgh Courier's* Fab 40 awardees. In 2014, she was accepted into the Pittsburgh Filmmaker's Flight School, a professional development program for artists, where she began to expand her art beyond music and explore working with other media such as glass, wood, and found objects. In 2018, Amber received *Pittsburgh Magazine's* 40 Under 40 award. She is also a member of the #notwhite collective, a group of thirteen women who are bi/multi-racial/culture, immigrants, or descendants of immigrants who have come together to question, investigate, and dig deep into what identity is within and without the construct and context of white supremacy and do not align themselves with society's system of oppression. Amber looks forward to continuing the work that she is doing in both the higher education sector as well as the arts world and the communities that she is involved in, hoping to find innovative ways to encourage people to cross boundaries in order to create, learn, and grow.

Elaine Frantz is a Professor of History at Kent State University, who has been a proud member of the Elsinore Bennu Think Tank for Restorative Justice for many years. She is the author of two books: *Manhood Lost: Drunken Men and Redeeming Women in the Nineteenth Century United States* (Johns Hopkins University Press, 2002) and *Ku-Klux: The Birth of the Klan in the Reconstruction Era* (University of North Carolina Press, 2016). She is writing a third book, about the history of paid violence work in Pittsburgh. She has published academic articles in the *Journal of American History*, the *Journal of Southern History*, and the *Journal of Social History* and popular pieces in *We're History* and *Vox*. She has been interviewed by *Backstory* and BBC-4, and for pieces in Slate. She lives with her remarkably sane partner, her two formidable teenagers, and her two unreasonably demanding cats.

Christine Lorenz is an artist who uses photography, and sometimes text. She teaches the history of art and visual culture at Duquesne University, and also teaches writing to photographers at Point Park University. She holds an MFA from the University of California, Santa Barbara, and lives with her family in Pittsburgh.

Fly (James Martin) is a prisoner with over thirty-five years in the Pennsylvania prison system. During the course of his incarceration he has continued to strive to better his self. He helped start the first ever Police Training Inside-Out course inside a prison. He is a member of the Elsinore Bennu Think Tank for Restorative Justice. In prison, he works as a Certified Peer Specialist helping other prisoners get along.

Shawn (Clarence) Robinson was born September 30, 1968 to a sixteen-year-old mother, Elizabeth, and a twenty-year-old father, Clarence Sr. He was born at Magee Women's Hospital in Pittsburgh. His biological father went to prison for twenty years when he was around five years old. His mother raised him and his younger sister alone until she met his stepfather, John. Then his younger brother, John III, was born. They lived in Penn Hills until they got a divorce when he was ten. He stayed with his stepfather and brother after the divorce. Around age fourteen, he went to live with his mother. At sixteen, he dropped out of school and went to Job Corps, but got kicked out after nine months for fighting. After Job Corps, he started getting into trouble with breaking the law. His mother could not handle him so she gave him the option to move out, which he did at age sixteen, living alone in Northview Heights, a housing project on Pittsburgh's north side. He started breaking into stores to make money, which lead him to serve three years in prison when he was nineteen to twenty-one. He tried to work when he first got home from prison in 1991, but his criminal record made it hard to find and keep a job. After three months, he started selling drugs, first crack and, two months later, heroin. He met the mother of his daughter in 1991 and they dated until 1993 when he went to jail for murder. He found out while he was fighting his case that his girlfriend was pregnant with his only child. His daughter was born in June 1994. Two months later, he was convicted of first-degree murder. From 1996 on, out of love for his daughter, he changed his lifestyle and started to become a better person. Now he is trying to "earn" his way out of prison through commutation. The end is yet to be determined.

Nechama Weingart is a licensed social worker in Pittsburgh, Pennsylvania. She holds a Bachelor's and a Master's degree in Social Work from Cleveland State University. She works as a reentry program specialist and therapist for the Institute for Justice Research & Development, improving reentry outcomes for formerly incarcerated individuals. She is also a medical advocate with Pittsburgh Action Against Rape and a member of the Elsinore Bennu Think Tank. Nechama has a particular interest in trauma, and has experience with a variety of trauma-related services. She has worked with refugees, survivors of human trafficking and domestic violence, and families involved in the child welfare system. When not helping others, Nechama enjoys the company of books, friends, dogs, the forest, and adventures.

John Edgar Wideman's books include *American Histories, Writing to Save a Life, Philadelphia Fire, Brothers and Keepers, Fatheralong,*

Hoop Dreams, and *Sent for You Yesterday.* He is a MacArthur Fellow, has won the PEN/Faulkner Award twice, and has twice been a finalist for the National Book Critics Circle Award and National Book Award. He divides his time between New York and France.

Faruq (Robert Douglas Wideman) was born on December 29, 1950, to Bettie and Edgar Wideman, the youngest of five children: his siblings are John, Otis, Letisha, and David. He graduated high school in Pittsburgh, and earned an associate's degree from Allegheny Community College and several additional college credits from the University of Pittsburgh before they closed their prison education program. Mr. Wideman had two sons: Omar and Chance.